P9-CMF-642

261
T42W

THE WORKING CHURCH.

THE

Working Church.

BY

CHARLES F. THWING, D.D.,

AUTHOR OF "AMERICAN COLLEGES: THEIR STUDENTS AND WORK."
"THE READING OF BOOKS;" AND JOINT AUTHOR OF
"THE FAMILY: AN HISTORICAL AND
SOCIAL STUDY;" ETC.

REVISED EDITION.

NEW YORK
THE BAKER AND TAYLOR CO.
33-37 EAST SEVENTEENTH ST., UNION SQ. NORTH

TO

The Two Churches

I HAVE LOVED AND SERVED AS MINISTER:

THE NORTH AVENUE CONGREGATIONAL, OF CAMBRIDGE,

AND

THE PLYMOUTH, OF MINNEAPOLIS.

CONTENTS.

.*. Parts of several of the chapters have been published
in such journals as the "Independent," "Christian Union,"
"Congregationalist," and "Advance."

THE WORKING CHURCH.

CHAPTER I.

CHURCH AND PASTOR. — INTRODUCTORY.

THE Church is at once the church of the Son of God and the church of the Son of Man. It is the church of the Son of God. He is its head; He is its Spirit, and it is His body; He is its life. Its origin is in the principle of divine love embodied in Him. Its history is the history of the unveiling of the principle of human redemption. The church is the church of the Son of Man. It includes all those who accept the principle of divine love, and endeavor to obey the duties revealed by this love. It includes all those who are "predestinated," says

Wycliffe. It embraces all holding the Word and observing the sacraments, says Luther. It is the visible organization in which pure doctrine is taught, says Melanchthon. It is a society in which every regenerate soul is a component part, says Schleiermacher. It is the religious community into which civil society grows in its moral development, suggests Rothe. The Church, therefore, is at once divine and human, — divine in origin, divine in continued dependence on divine grace, divine in the glorious consummation which awaits its development; human in including mankind, and in having as its sphere of activity the whole world. Down to the Reformation of the sixteenth century the Church was considered primarily as a divine institution; in the last three hundred years its human relations have, with each passing generation, become more conspicuous.

It is to the human relations of the Church that this book is devoted. Of these human relations only the more aggressive are included within its view.

The work of Christ's redemption is continued by His Church. The labor of the Church, therefore, is primarily the turning of men from sin unto righteousness. Its purpose is the incarnation of holiness in the individual and in the community. The field of this labor embraces all classes, ages, and conditions.

Its prime duty is the conversion to, and edification in, Christ of those who are within its immediate relation ; but it also bears relations to the universal cause of Christ, and owes duties to philanthropy. It is the great missionary power. It is to obey the command of going forth and evangelizing the world. Missionary endeavor — local, national, universal — is its simple duty, and is also its increasing joy. Its members should heed the individual call of the consecration of their lives and of their wealth to this service. Every form of wise charity it should seek to foster ; it should strive to inspire charity with the spirit of Christ, and to impress it with the methods of Christian self-helpfulness. It is itself a temperance organization, and should co-operate with every wise endeavor for ridding the home and the nation of the direful curse of drunkenness. It should strive to teach labor its dignity and duties, and capital its responsibilities and worthy rights. It should seek to dispel poverty by removing its causes, giving not alms so much as friendship. It should welcome every wise attempt to construct the social order upon a better basis than the present, yet disavowing all regard for a godless communism. It should show to the working-man that every movement toward a free Sunday is a movement toward a working Sunday. It should, in general, prove itself a friend to every man whom it can help to make more worthy of the Christ who died for him.

The sphere of the Church is as broad as the world : its work is limited only by the needs of sinning, suffering humanity ; its duty is measured only by its power, in the name of Christ, of serving and saving lost men. In its relation to other churches of the same or other order, the individual church is to be guided by the principles of Christian liberty and courtesy. Laboring for the public weal, it is never to strive to build itself through the decline of other worthy interests. It is to recognize that the prosperity of all churches and the prosperity of common interests and objects are more worthy than its own individual growth. Yet it is always to labor to make itself vigorous, strong, and efficient, for the sake of Him to whom it belongs and whom it serves, and for the sake of the world He would save.

The pastor of a church holds to it a twofold relation, — that of preacher and of chief executive officer. The preaching should be devoted to the promotion of Christian character. Its content and burden should be the gospel. Its methods should be adapted to the intellectual and other conditions of those to whom it is addressed. Its tone should be invariably warm, earnest, and spiritual. It should embrace the doctrines, and should also be intensely practical in aim and application. It should be supported by the Bible, and should prove itself true and just to human reason. It should be convincing in argument and persuasive in appeal. It should be the truth of God known in the life of the preacher, making itself known to other lives. It should be at once, in the broadest and narrowest sense, Christian.

The executive work of the pastor is as broad and diverse as the work of the church. But his chief purpose is to develop the activities of his church as a Christian institution. He is, therefore, to plan methods and to suggest lines of Christian service; to stimulate energy; to adjust work to worker, and worker to work. He is to unite individuals into co-operative labor. He is also to attempt to allot to each member some specific and individual Christian service. He is to work through workers. Yet he should be ashamed to spare himself. In his general bearing he is to be a bishop, overseeing the individual lives of the members; a shepherd in the older meaning, leading and not driving his flock, loving and trying to show himself worthy of being loved, trusting and trusted, as he may merit ; a minister, rejoicing in every opportunity of service for his Master among men. In a larger and more public relation he should not fail to conceive and to do his duty to the cause of education, embodied in school and college, endeavoring to make it Christian ; never, moreover, should he forget that he is a citizen of a Commonwealth whose founders regarded the Church and the State as one.

But if the pastor is a minister of the church, he is also, and more, a minister of, and for, and by Christ. Like the disciples on the Mount of Transfiguration, he is to see no man "save Jesus only." The truth of Christ he is to know, the duty of Christ to do, and the commendation of Christ to endeavor to receive.

CHAPTER II.

THE course of study in the theological seminaries has been greatly enlarged within a decade. Biblical theology, archæology, languages cognate to the Hebrew, and science in its relation to religion, have found a place in the curriculum. Essential as some teachers regard these studies to the complete scholarly equipment of the minister, they are yet not as essential as a subject in which little or no instruction is given. This subject relates to the administrative or executive work of a church. In one sense this department is akin to what is usually called pastoral theology; in another sense it is quite remote. As pastoral theology has been taught, it consists of the barest commonplaces and insipid platitudes. My

own studies at a theological school are not
so distant that my memory of them is in-
distinct; but the chief fact in the course
of lectures on pastoral theology — delivered
by a most godly and lovable professor, now of
blessed memory — which I yet recall, is that
a pastor should not, under ordinary conditions, make a call of more than twenty minutes. Instructions as to the performance of
a marriage or the conduct of a funeral service
or the leading of a prayer-meeting are not
by any manner of means to be despised ; but
such instructions are no more adequate to the
demands which the young minister is asked
to meet, than the old spinning-wheel is capable
of furnishing thread for the modern loom.

The problem which every young minister
meets in his installation over a church is this:
What can be done to put this church to work?
What can be done to cause it to impress
Christian sentiment upon this community ?
What can I, its pastor, do to make this
church a power? How shall I work with
it ? His sermons may be biblical, eloquent,

instructive, inspiring ; his pastoral visits re-
lentless in their systematic thoroughness ;
his leadership of the devotional meetings
wise : but all this, *his* work, does not quicken
the church to its work. Over and above all
this, are several departments or sections of
church work which he should organize and
formulate, and for the organization and formu-
lation of which the training of the theological
school should give him aid.

The training of the baptized children in
the truths and duties of the covenant which
their parents have made in their behalf ; the
training also of all the children in a knowledge of the Bible and of Christian doctrine ;
the ways and means of conducting classes in
some catechism or synopsis of biblical truth ;
the work with, for, and through the young men
and women of the parish, — their organization for aggressive labor, sympathy with them
in the difficulties besetting the first years of
Christian experience, and the methods of
arousing and guiding their enthusiasm ; the
ways and means for reaching the unchurched,

— the character of the popular Sunday-evening service, the neighborhood prayer-meeting, the open-air meeting of the Sabbath afternoon in the city, the reaching the back districts in the country through school-house Sunday-schools, prayer-meetings, and preaching services ; the work for the intemperate, for the young in reference to temperance, sewing-schools, cooking-schools, and similar philanthropic agencies ; special endeavors to restore lapsed church-members ; assigning special church work to each new member ; the introduction of the new families joining the congregation to the older families ; methods of greeting and interesting strangers in the church ; the Sunday-school in all its manifold interests of the instruction of teacher and pupil, of division into departments and classes, of keeping vigorous the spiritual side of the teaching ; the organization of mission schools, — all these, and many more features and departments, the young pastor, immediately after his first service on the Sabbath, is called to consider. A minister of large common sense, without previous training, will attack the problem and solve it to the best of his ability. But many ministers will be either unconscious that any such problem is before them, or will be inclined to sit down before it with hands folded.

The solution of the religious problem of the city lies in the administration of the church. So, also, does the solution of the equally important religious problem of the country. No class of professional men is working more hours each week, or working more severely than the clerical. The surprise is that their sermons are as good as they are. The seminaries train students well, never better, for doing their individual work of writing helpful sermons. To the sermon I would assign the highest place in Christian instruction and inspiration. But the minister should know that his chief executive work is to make other people work. He can do little, very little himself, to lessen misery, to arouse religious conviction, and to convert the city or the village to sound views or righteous prac-

tice. He should read carefully the lesson
of his inability and limitations. But he also
should know that through others the little
one himself may become a thousand. Let
him be the commander-in-chief, not to fight
himself, but to train others for fighting, to
plan the campaign and put these trained
workers into the field of action. The
churches — that is, the individual members
of the churches — are to do Christ's work.
The pastor is the chief of directors. The
most useful church is the most laborious
church. Not less preaching, but more ; not
less learning, but more ; not less eloquence,
but more ; but above all present human in-
struments, ability to put a church to work in
its community, is the need.

Various definitions are given of the Church,
according as the Church is conceived as local
or universal, denominational or catholic, visible or invisible ; but these various definitions have one common element, a belief in
Christ as the Saviour of the world. It would
be well, I think, if our conception of the

Church could be so formulated as expressly to include, not simply those believing in Christ as the world's Saviour, but also those who are laboring to bring the world unto Christ to be saved. The Church is the collective body of those who are endeavoring to serve Christ among men. The idea of the Church as a working force needs reiterated emphasis. For the Church is the incarnate Christ, and is to continue and to complete the work which He came to begin. The Church is the evangelizing, missionary power. The mission of the Holy Ghost we are to honor and to co-operate with ; but with His purpose of leading into all truth and of sanctifying men, we are in closest union when we obey the command of Him who sent the Holy Spirit, the command to "go." The Roman Catholic Church has its order of workers ; but in the Protestant Church each member is supposed to be a worker. Wesley's motto, with slight variations, is right : "All at it, at all times, in all places, and in all ways." We should not have simply the church of Saint

Paul, the church holding forth the faith; neither should we have simply the church of Saint James, on whose front works are blazoned; but we should have the Church of Christ, in which neither faith nor works are neglected, but in which both are harmoniously united and effectively adjusted. It is, therefore, evident that the Church of Christ is the Church at work in Christ's service.

To the church thus at work the pastor holds the relation of bishop, overseer, president, director, guide. He is himself to be a laborious worker. He cannot hope to have his church at work, unless he is at once an example and an inspiration. If he be laborious; cordial to strangers and new families; attentive to the sick, the mourning, and the poor; wisely regular in his parochial labor; thoughtful of those requiring special watch and ward, as the new convert and the inquirer; strong, vigorous, aggressive, eager to do as much as possible, — his church will catch the enthusiasm of his example, and will be aroused by the inspiration of his work.

Choose the churches in New York, Chicago, Boston, Philadelphia, which are most active and aggressive, and it will be found, with scarcely an exception, that they are the churches manned by the most active, aggressive, and laborious ministers. The old minister said to the young minister, "If you are a faithful minister of Jesus Christ, you will have many an aching head, weary back, and heavy heart." Yes ; the minister's head ought to ache, and his back ought to be weary, and his heart ought to be heavy, in the noble and devoted earnestness of his labor. As a class, ministers are more laborious than lawyers or doctors ; but most ministers should be far more devoted to the work. If they cannot be Pauls, they can be Paul-like in the enthusiasm, courage, and persistency of their work.

In arousing his church to its work and in securing workers, the pastor will receive aid by making the tone of his preaching missionary and evangelizing. The conception of the Church as a collective body of Christians laboring in Christ's cause should be almost as constant an element in each sermon as the statement of the terms of salvation. He should seek to indoctrinate his hearers with the gospel of work. This general character of his preaching will not prevent him from occasionally devoting special sermons to special departments or demands. But beside this method and principle, each pastor should personally and individually call men to special service. Knowing the work which God seems to ordain his Church to do, alert to discover those who may serve in this divinely appointed mission, he should be as the chaplain of St. Andrews who summoned John Knox into the Christian ministry: "I charge thee, as thou hast a regard for the glory of God, the salvation of men, and your own eternal well-being, that you neglect not this duty to which God calls."

The pastor can and may in God's name summon men to service in the Sabbath-school, to service in gathering in the un-churched, to service in establishing missions, to service in the cause of charity, to service in any one of the lines of endeavor by which the Church seeks to move the world.

Though no member is to be indifferent to any part of the work of the church, each member has abilities which more efficiently qualify him for service in one part than in another. The dictate of common sense and the dictate of the Scripture is that he devote his powers to those lines of work in which they will prove of most worth. One man, with a peculiar readiness of address, may be ordained by the pastor for looking after the unchurched and the new families taking up their residence in the neighborhood of the church. To one woman may be committed the special task of gathering children into the Sunday-school. To another woman may be intrusted the duty of instructing the children in the Bible, in a way more thorough than the hour of the Sabbath-school permits. The charitable work, not in the negative sense of giving away old clothes or sending out dozens of Thanksgiving turkeys, but in the positive sense of showing one's self a genuine friend to those in need, may be commended to the wise diligence of a special board of ladies and gentlemen. The work, too, of instructing the young men and women in the Bible and in Christian doctrine and in matters of church work should be placed in the special charge of those competent for this serious duty. The outlook committee on mission work, local, national, foreign, should not fail of receiving consideration.

The pastor, seeing the work which his church ought to do, understanding so far as possible the abilities of its members, should seek to set each member to that task to which nature and grace have fitted him. His worthy purpose is to put others to work. He may in the first year of his pastorate work much harder in getting his church to work than he would in doing himself all the work which he gets it to do ; but it is better for the church always, and in the end better for himself, that this division and subdivision of labor be pursued. Let the pastor himself train special workers for special works. Agassiz was once asked what was his greatest work in Ameriea. His reply was, the training of three men. "One," said the great naturalist, "has abandoned my theories, and one has become indifferent to me ; but the scientific training of three scholars is my greatest work," — greater than the building of the great museum at Cambridge, greater than all the investigations on two continents which made him one of the first naturalists of the century. Likewise many a pastor finds his greatest work in a ministry, not the building of a splendidly equipped meeting-house, not the receiving even of hundreds into church-fellowship, but the conversion to Christ and the training of a few men and women who are thus qualified for eminent service. Let each pastor know the work which his church is evidently by its position ordained of God to do. Let him, with this knowledge, study to allot this work in its diverse forms to those who can and ought to do it.

Having secured his co-workers, the pastor is to train them for effective labor. In most instances these whom he thus invites are in greater or less need of instruction and discipline in church work. The work itself is the best training-school, but he may himself give them aid. The more than four hundred missionaries of the London City Mission receive a training more or less peculiarly fitted to their peculiar duties. The instruction which a pastor gives may be special and individual; but the main purpose which qualifies all his teaching is to teach the use of the Bible in bringing the unconverted to Christ. In following this aim he will give instruction in the Scriptures, and in particular in the fundamental truths of the Scriptures. He will illustrate and emphasize his meanings by the use of actual instances of conversion. God the Father, God the Saviour, God the Holy Ghost, grace, repentance, forgiveness, confession, faith, regeneration, conversion, justification, are subjects which he considers in the light of the Bible. In the study of individual

cases he will seek to show how the Word,
"fitly spoken" and "in season," has proved
to be the "sword of the Spirit," sharper than a
"two edged-sword, piercing even to the divid-
ing asunder of soul and spirit . . . and a dis-
cerner of the thoughts and intents of the
heart." He will endeavor to give suggestions as to dealing with the doubter, the ignorant, the fearful, the discouraged, the wilful,
the complaining, the proud, those lacking conviction, those lacking decision, those weak in
the faith, backsliders, and new converts.
Thus, month by month, year by year, training his associates to service, he tries to equip
them for the general or particular duties to
which nature and grace seem to call them.

CHAPTER III.

THE WORTH AND THE WORTHLESSNESS
OF METHODS.

EVERY pastor has his methods in working with and for his church, and in getting his church to work. The exact nature of these methods is of less importance than the fact that the methods are his own, — methods with which he is acquainted and which he can handle. Ecclesiastical methods, like personal habits, are constitutional. If they are not his own, if he fails to understand them, he is quite as helpless as David in Goliath's armor, or as Goliath with David's sling and stones. In his use of methods of work the pastor is exposed to perils.

Among these perils is the danger of believing that methods which are successful in one

church will prove successful in another, or
that methods which succeed in a church at
one time will always succeed. Methods should
be very elastic. They should be capable of
great adaptiveness. They should be adjusted
to the peculiar needs of each church. For
instance, the prayer-meeting should be a
meeting for, and of, and by the people. But
a church may for generations have been accustomed to regard this meeting as a lecture
by the minister. The newly installed pastor,
with memories of the pleasant conferences of
his former charge, cannot transform the hour
of a lecture given by one into an hour of
religious conversation shared in by a score.
Moreover, the type of the prayer-meeting in
which religious conversation prevails may in
time become vapid and inconsequential. The
pastor should endeavor to throw greater intellectual vigor into its exercises without diminishing their heartiness. In every respect a
pastor should hold himself ready to surrender
or to alter his methods according to the demands of the place or the time.

In thus doing, the pastor is guarded from a not uncommon peril, — namely, of believing that methods have intrinsic worth. Of course we all know that they are good only so far forth as they do good; yet long associations with methods may result in transferring our regard for the end to the means by which the end is gained. Systematic pastoral visitation is an idol with not a few ministers; but the annual or biennial call on each family is not an ideal which is to be followed inflexibly without reference to the real needs of any family, or to the good which a pastor may do by special attention to certain households. Each minister is to put his pastoral or his other work in that place where it will effect the richest results.

In subordinating methods to ends, aid may be drawn from keeping constantly before the mind and heart the supreme aim of all church work, — the development of Christian character. If any method fails to achieve this purpose, it is useless; if it succeeds in achieving this purpose, it has value. Every method should be brought to this ultimate test of conversion and edification. No matter how perfect the machinery of a church, or how admirably and noiselessly or boisterously it moves, if it fails here it is a complete failure. We must maintain this aim as ultimate and supreme, and cause methods to adjust themselves to this ideal. This most worthy purpose elevates toil, ennobles self-sacrifice, adjusts difficulties, eliminates selfishness, strengthens patience, gives to work enthusiasm and enlargement, and crowns it with increasing success.

A pastor should also guard himself from the danger of imposing his methods on churches unwilling or indifferent to receive them. We ministers are not to have pet hobbies to impose on anybody, least of all on those whose servants we are. We are to justify the wisdom of what we propose to do in a church, and of the ways in which we hope to win our aim. This justification it is not necessary to herald in advance, if our purposes are right and our methods wise.

They will prove to be their own justification. It may be that a church to whose pastorate a minister is called, has methods and practices which are superior to any he may himself possess. In this case he should be more than willing to adopt these methods, and to work them to the best of his ability. Along this same line it is to be still further said that abrupt changes of method are usually evil. Churches, no more than children, like to be *jerked*. It is also worthy of remark that we young ministers in particular are in danger, in an adoption of church methods, of not showing sufficient deference to elders and to those who have special interest in the church. It may also be true that we are in peril of paying too much deference to the wealthy and scholarly classes. To avoid this peril of pastoral autocracy, the pastor should hold full and frequent conferences with the officers, and should not adopt important measures except with their approval and the promise of their hearty co-operation. For he is not lord or autocrat, but overseer, president, nay, the servant, of his church, and of him whom he calls Master.

It is further to be borne in mind that no method, however perfect, is a substitute for power. The method is only the way in which the intellectual, emotional, volitional, spiritual power is manifest. Method without power is a locomotive on the track without steam. Power without method is the locomotive with steam in the boiler and pipe, but derailed and ploughing its path to its own destruction. Power manifests itself in method, but method is no substitute for power. Nothing takes the place of a real love on the part of the pastor for his people. If he fails to love them, the wisest of methods will succeed in winning only a partial success. If he loves them, his best methods will succeed more thoroughly by reason of his love ; and his indifferent methods will prove of some worth. "My little children, I write unto you that ye love one another."

CHAPTER IV.

AMONG THE CHILDREN.

HILDREN should be constantly trained to love Jesus and to feel His love. Character sets early. Life-long tendencies are indicated in the first years. In his autobiography Darwin says that in his early boyhood he had a passion for collecting all sorts of things. Shells, seals, francs, coins, and minerals were among the objects he gathered. We have now fewer juvenile prodigies than formerly; but on the whole, character is fixed at an earlier age. The boy is not only the father of the man; the boy *is* the man. Evil begins to train its children early for its service. A boy of four-teen was lately hanged in Texas for murder. A lad whom I knew was accused of an infamous crime. When his mother was told of it

she said, " Why, it is not possible! Arthur is
only a little baby." Children grow old in
wickedness before they reach their teens, and
while their mothers think they are as inno-
cent as infants. Heathendom trains its children early. As soon as a pagan boy is strong
enough to hold a flower in his hand, he is
taught to lay that flower at the feet of an
idol. The Roman Catholic Church trains its
children early. Every mother entering the
church with her baby in her arms puts the
holy water upon the baby's forehead.

From the earliest years children should be
trained to love Jesus and to feel His love.
Thomas Chalmers was so thoroughly trained
in this respect, that from his first years he de-
clared his purpose to become a minister. It
is told that Edward Payson, when he was not
more than three years old, would often weep
under the preaching of the gospel, and would
sometimes call his mother to his bedside to
talk with him as to his soul's salvation. Such
an experience is abnormal: it ought to be
discouraged; it is neither healthy nor health-

ful. But it is normal for the boy of ten, like Leonard Woods, — the first Professor of Theology at Andover, where he continued for a quarter of a century, — to desire to be educated for Christian service.

Tertullian made a remark which has become famous : "Man is naturally Christian." In one respect the remark is false; in another it is true. The remark is true, in that the child heart loves Jesus. The child "takes to" Christ. The story of Christ's love awakens the child's loyalty; and the story of Christ's death, the child's indignation. Next to the love for father and mother, nay, beyond, beneath, and around the love for mother and for father, the child from the first should be taught to love Jesus. There should be no need of conversion and turning about. The curve in an ascending spiral, not a right angle, should represent the Christian's development. Children should never know the time when they did not love Jesus. The saintly Baxter was at one period greatly troubled because he could not recollect the

hour when there was a gracious change in
his character; but at last he discovered that
education is as properly the means of grace
as preaching. Thus he found comfort sweeter
in his love for Christ, because he could not
remember the time when he did not love
Him.

A distinguished clergyman now living
writes in charming style of his early Christian life. Such a story as he tells should be
far more common than it is : —

"My earliest memory is a religious memory. In
my home the entire atmosphere was persistently
religious. I learned to read so young that I have
no recollection whatever of the process, and the
daily reading of the Bible was as much a part of my
young life as the daily breakfast. With sweet and
steady pressure, and at the same time with a pressure wonderfully wise, my mother was always leading, referring, forcing me to Jesus. I can think of
no time when, because of her enwrapping teaching,
I did not recognize myself a sinner, and did not, in
a boyish way at least, look to Christ as Saviour.
Her steady test for things by which she taught me
to decide concerning this or that was, Would it

please Jesus? When I had done wrong, — and I did wrong by no means infrequently, — though I might repent toward her and ask her forgiveness, I was always taught that the finishing of the matter had never come until I had personally sorrowed toward and asked forgiveness of the Lord. So Christ hung as a sun steadily and consciously to myself in all my childish horizon. To please my parents was a sweet thing, I was taught; but to please Christ and my parents for His sake, a sweeter thing. Yet there was no cant in all this, nor the least sanctimoniousness. It seemed to be all as natural and right to me as breathing. So, really, I cannot remember the time when I did not look upon the Lord Jesus as my personal Saviour, did not trust Him, did not recognize and accept it as the task of life to serve Him."

The proposition, therefore, is evident that children should be constantly trained to love Jesus and to feel His love for them.

If any period of half a dozen years in the life of a child be more critical, religiously, than any other, it is the six years following the age of ten. At this age the boys and girls usually are graduated from the primary department of the Sunday-school into its intermediate or higher department. If they have received proper instruction, many of them are at this time Christians. If I need not seek evidence beyond my own early boyhood to prove the doctrine of total depravity, I also need not seek evidence beyond the limits of my first pastorate, to prove that the hearts of many young children are inclined to accept Jesus as their guide, helper, Saviour. They, at an early age, know somewhat of the evil of sin. They appreciate, even more than many who are their seniors, the tenderness of the love of Christ. They affirm their love of Jesus. They are willing to promise to try to be and to do as they believe He desires. Their homes and school-rooms and play-grounds bear witness to the reality of their endeavor. Their wills are moved, their intellects are also enlightened, and their feelings touched. "Except ye become as little children:" they have no need of becoming; they are little children. They are essential Christians. They have not an "experience" such as their elders

have. They ought not to have ; they cannot have it. But they are able to endure
the test which our Lord applied to Peter at
the close of His divine mission, "Lovest thou
me ? " They are in kind as truly Christians
at the age of ten, after a few years of proper
instruction, as they are at the age of seventy ;
as the child who is studying his " first
reader" is as really reading as the scholar
who is perusing Gibbon's polished and well-
rounded sentences.

But with children thus circumstanced and
inclined at the age of ten, the following
four or five years work tremendous changes.
They have fallen from grace. They have become, if not hard and hardened, indifferent
and careless. Their attention to Christian
truth is not easily secured. The heart is not
quite so soft as before. They reason, inquire,
in a way doubt. The fact is, their suscepti-
bility to spiritual impressions has diminished.
They feel the downward gravitation of the
world, the flesh, and the devil. Their love
for Christ is either dying or dead.

In this common condition the problem which the church has set before it is this: to keep these child-Christians from falling from their first love between the critical years of ten and sixteen; to foster the spirit of Christian character; to strengthen the weak hope; to educate and discipline the imperfect faith. For the solution of this serious problem we may look for aid to the Sunday-school teacher. If he is wise, faithful, earnest, we do not look to him in vain. But in too many instances he fails to have the power or the time essential for this work. It is a surprise, in view of the lack of proper method in the choice of teachers in the Sunday-school, that the Sunday-school accomplishes so great results. As now constituted, however, the Sunday-school in its main department is seldom nurturing to a natural maturity the Christian character which is born before the child reaches the age of ten.

In this failure, what can be done? I write out of my own experience when I say that

a special class should be formed of those
young Christians, and that special instruction and guidance should be given them.
This instruction and guidance should be committed to one most able to give it. This one
may be the pastor, or it may not be. If it is
not he, he should discover some other person
qualified to perform this duty. I think I may
say that the pastor will usually find that it is
wise to intrust this labor to other hands; and
yet these other hands he may think it well
specially to train for this important service.
This instruction should consist of a systematic presentation of the great truths of
Christ. It should be systematic, taking up
in order the central doctrines and themes
of the Bible. It should be, it must be, to secure favorable results, attractive,— attractive
in the person of the teacher and attractive
in its methods. It should be thorough; for
children will receive and appreciate, be it
properly illustrated, Christian teaching far
more profound than is commonly credited to
them. Such a class should meet on some

week-day, after the close of the exercises of the public school, and should be held each week for certain periods of each year.

With the methods and the results of such teaching, I am already somewhat acquainted. Year by year I have seen a class of boys and girls grow from a membership of forty to a membership of three hundred. I have seen these boys and girls listening intently to the presentation of the historic facts and truths of the Bible. I have seen this class made so attractive that scores of children would *run* from the public school-room to the church school-room in order to lose no moment of the short hour. I have seen this interest aroused and maintained by the power of a strong and living personality rather than by extraneous aids. I know this teaching to be systematic and thorough. I have seen examination papers in writing of these boys and girls that were a wonder in their revelation of the appreciation of the nature and duties of the Christian life. I have been made glad in receiving many of those thus trained into the membership of the church, and have daily rejoiced in beholding the good confessions they witnessed at home and school. The church may aid in such training of children by receiving them into its membership. I know of no help so great which the home may receive, I know of no help so great which the child may receive beyond the walls of the home, as the help which the church may thus give. Such a confession in the church of Christ brings to the surface and crystallizes all the child's love for his Saviour. It furnishes him with a high exterior standard of conduct ; it puts him in that direct line of which the end, as is also the beginning, is life eternal.

The Christian child needs the church to make his Christian love vivid, positive, aggressive. The Christian parent needs the church to aid in the Christian training of his Christian child. The church needs the Christian child, that its altars may never lack for Samuels, as its ministering priests. If the church is a family, it must specially care

for its children. If the church is Christ's
church, it must specially seek to bless those
whom He blessed. If the church is ever to
rejoice in its millennial triumph, it will include children, even little children, among
its disciples and apostles.

Various objections are urged to children
becoming members of a church. These
objections, however, are in large measure
founded upon misconceptions of the need
of the child or of the duty of the church.
One of the more common of these objections
is that the child does not fully understand
the meaning of a public confession. It is true
that a child does not fully understand this
step ; but who of us, of whatever age, does
fully understand? Are we not often asking
our children to take important steps, the
meaning of which is not fully understood?
How much does a child need to understand
to join the church ? How much does an
adult need to understand ? Has the reader
fathomed more than a small part of the doctrines of the creed ? Who has reached final

conclusions in all his thinking? Has God's Word ceased to break forth with new light? What did Philip require of the eunuch as a condition of baptism? "And the eunuch said, See, here is water; what doth hinder me to be baptized? and Philip saith, If thou believest with all thine heart, thou mayest. And he answered and said, I believe that Jesus Christ is the Son of God." Philip baptized him.

A class of girls in the church was recently asked to write out their answers to the question, "What is it to be a Christian?" Among the answers were these: A girl of fifteen said, "It is to believe that the Saviour is able to save us, that He will forgive us; it is to love the Saviour and try to do His will." A girl of thirteen replied, "To be a Christian is to love and serve the Lord, and try to do as much as you can, and live as near Him as you can." A girl also of thirteen said, "It is to try to be good and do good, and to love Jesus Christ." A girl of fifteen answered, "To be a Christian is to love Jesus

4

Christ with your whole heart, and to yield your will to Him completely." One of thirteen gave this answer, which is remarkable as a philosophical definition of what it is to be a Christian : "To give one's whole being to the will of God."

It is not to be said that children do not understand more of wickedness than their parents desire. Children do understand more of goodness and more of Christian truth than their parents give them credit for.

It is also urged as an objection to children joining the church, that they may not hold out. A little girl said to me recently, " Why, if I join the church, I may go back." " Yes," I replied, "and you may go back if you don't join the church ; the church should be a help to keep you from going back." Do all those who are not children hold out ? I might select fifty boys and girls from the Sunday-school whom I thought suitable candidates for church-membership ; I might select fifty men and women from the congregation whom I thought also suitable candidates.

After five years I am confident I should find a larger proportion of the children than of the adults maintaining their Christian faith.

Two or three principles or methods underlie the Christian character and the church-membership of children. One is that the Christian life is of the individual character: being of the individual character, it is chiefly concerned with the feelings and the will: in children the feelings are strong and the will easily influenced: therefore, without full intellectual apprehension, the Christian life may begin in children.

The second principle is that the Christian life is a growth, not a manufactured product; a flower, not a machine: therefore, for its purest and noblest development, it must begin early.

It is also evident that for the Christian life of children parents are in a large measure responsible. The method, as some one has said, is to "make a young person love you, and then simply being in his presence will make him what you want him to be." The "experience" of the child so far as he is concerned is slight, but it is important so far as the mother or the father is concerned. As one has said, writing of his mother : "She put my little hand in the hand of the Lord Jesus. I did not know what else to do, and so I clasped His hand,— that was all. But if I ever stand yonder in the great shining, about the sole reason, on the human side, will be— *my mother*. God bless her!"

CHAPTER V.

AMONG THE YOUNG PEOPLE.

DEPARTMENT of the administration of the church in which the pastor finds it well to have peculiar interest, is the work among those who are universally known as the "young people." The "young people" have within a generation come to occupy a most important place in the church. To work among them for their conversion and edification, to work for them fitting them for Christian service, and to work through them in the manifold endeavor of the church, no one is better qualified than the pastor. The systematic organization of this body for work in the church is to be greatly desired. These young men and women usually lend themselves more easily than their elders to organization and to organized effort. Many of them desire Christian work. They have fewer prejudices and less individuality. They are not heavily laden with the cares of business or of home. They are less conservative, more progressive. They also need the Christian training of systematic planning for, and systematic doing of, service. For the good of the church as well as their own good, this organization is to be fostered. Many a pastor finds that the most prompt, the most thorough, the most earnest, the most persistent, and the most satisfactory work of his church is done through the young people. They are his aids quite as truly as the members of the church committee.

This general movement among and for young people has taken positive shape in the Young People's Society of Christian Endeavor. Its great growth justifies its wisdom of administration, as well as proves its need. In nine years it has increased to include more than eight thousand organizations, embracing some five hundred thousand, or more, members. It is simply the young people of

the individual church associated for the purpose of promoting their Christian growth and
of bringing those not Christians to Christ.
Its methods are simple. Frequent testimony
in the weekly meeting is emphasized. Attendance at this service is obligatory. Social,
literary, and musical interests are grouped
about the central principles of Christian
growth and Christian service. Committees on
various departments — such as the Sunday-
school, the visiting of the sick and the crimi-
nal, the introduction of strangers, the care for
the prayer-meetings — are selected. A full
corps of the other customary officers forms a
part of the society. Membership is of two
classes, — the active, embracing those who
believe themselves to be Christians; and the
associate, including those who may wish to
enjoy certain privileges of the Society but are
not prepared to be known as Christians.

So familiar are the general principles and
methods of this movement, that it is unnecessary for me to say more in exposition. But it
may be fitting to add that in every church in

which the Society of Christian Endeavor has been established, it has proved to be the most satisfactory way for organizing its young people for Christian work. In not a few churches it has given birth to a prayer-meeting for young people ; in others it has quadrupled the attendance and increased the interest of this meeting ; in others it has proved to be the most laborious and the most effective of all the means and methods of church administration. In churches in which this general form of work among the young people is well planned and executed, it may or may not be wise at once to transfer a prosperous young people's organization into a society of this distinctive name ; but it is certainly true that God has not in this generation in America given a wiser method for the doing of Christian work for and through young people. Every church which is not thus organized among its younger members is neither availing itself of its strength nor entering into its waiting opportunities.

For the Young People's Society of Christian Endeavor, or any organization of young people, is not an association outside of the church. Undoubtedly any such alliance may be so formed or conducted as to give the impression of either rivalry or antagonism to the church. But it ought never to be so formed or conducted. It is simply the church at work among, and for, and through its younger members. It is not to be doubted that this peril exists. It is the peril of clique and faction. It is a peril which may result in direct opposition to the church. The younger members, feeling that the older have little interest in their work, go by themselves ; the older members, thinking that their juniors prefer to be by themselves, do not frequent their devotional or social meetings. Such a division is lamentable. It should always be avoided; it should, when existing, be healed. The younger members should know that the church is more than their society, and that of the church their society is a part or function. The older members, by sympathy most cordial and by endeavors for co-operative service, should prove that they rejoice in the activity and aggressiveness of their junior brethren.

In the organization of young people for church work, the religious basis must invariably be strongly maintained. No foundation, social, literary, musical, æsthetic, is either worthy or enduring. The young people themselves will accept of a constitution and method which are profoundly religious. Many of them even demand that a pre-eminently Christian character prevail in all their organized efforts. There is no need of hiding the Dover's powder of Christian service in the raspberry jam of "socials" or debates. Many of them find that Christian service is not a bitter thing, but very sweetness itself. Therefore let the centre and circumference of all organizing and of every organization be devoutly Christian; and on the radius may be put whatever of social enjoyment and of literary culture may seem fitting.

The church is a spiritual institution. Its means and methods, therefore, are determined

by its character as a spiritual institution.
Yet, though spiritual, it should be free to use
such indirect as well as direct agencies as
may contribute to the salvation of men from
sin. Some indirect agencies may be included
in the work of young people.

Among these agencies may be placed
popular amusements. Shall the church pro-
vide amusements for its young people? Shall
it countenance and nourish amusements which
it would not be expedient to admit into any
part of the church edifice? Is it wise for it
to erect a building in which games, such as
for example billiards, may be played? The
answer to these and allied questions depends
upon the influence of these diversions upon
the moral character of the young people. It
is the business of the church to minister to
this moral character. If the church is so
placed that it is necessary in order to catch
young people to use a billiard cue as a fishing-
rod, no hesitation should be felt in employ-
ing such an instrument. Churches situated
down town, and obliged to contend with

saloons as rallying-places for young men, may at times find it wise to use these measures. The church should be willing to adopt any method which will keep the young people away from evil associations. If it cannot secure the whole loaf of Christian character, let it secure the half-loaf of moral character; if it cannot secure the half-loaf, let it endeavor to secure as large an abstinence from evil as may be possible. The churches which bear the name of "People's Churches," and are attended by those less well-to-do, usually can minister in more ways to their members than churches composed of the wealthier classes. Such churches frequently find it advantageous to establish reading-rooms and parlors for the use of their members. Classes, too, for the instruction of the young people in stenography, needlework, and telegraphy prove of much worth. The church should have as one of its important aims the service of the young people of the church. This service should be as broad as the condition of the church and the need of the people allow. But in all service thus broad and sufficient, the highest aim should control the development of Christian manhood and womanhood.

The church working for its young folks should also put them to work. The older young people should give their hands and hearts and brains to philanthropic efforts, such as the distribution of books and newspapers in hospitals and jails, the holding of services of song in the wards of hospitals, the establishment and carrying on of Sunday-schools and gospel services in the mission stations of cities and in the schoolhouses in the country towns, and the holding of temperance meetings such as belong to the Bands of Hope for children. In all these and similar services the young people of the church may be made most efficient members of the working church.

CHAPTER VI.

AMONG BUSINESS MEN.

I VENTURE to recall a bit of personal experience. I was calling on my parishioners who do business in the Chamber of Commerce. Among those to whom I paid my respects was Mr. A. Mr. A. is still under forty; he is reputed to have large wealth, and to be making large additions to it. His commercial interests are various. His mind is keen, alert, vigorous; his heart is tender. He has all the best qualities of the best business man. As soon as I entered his office I saw that he was busy; I also saw, I was assured, that he was glad to see me. Presently he said, "You do not know how much good just your coming to see us does." I ventured to suggest that his sense of courtesy was getting the better of his sense of truthfulness. But he replied: "No; we men are from morning to night engaged in a hard struggle. I know that every man who enters that doorway comes to make some money out of me; and every man who enters that doorway I intend to make some money out of. It is more pleasant than I can tell you to see a man who you feel has some personal care for you, to see a man who looks upon you as something besides a mere money-maker, to see a man who represents something besides banks, real-estate syndicates, and elevator companies."

The earnestness of my friend's words and my knowledge of his character lead me to believe in their sincerity. They suggest the need of a Christian mission and the need of special spiritual endeavor for business men. The working church has been doing much for various classes, — for the children, for the young men, for the young women, for the outcast and wandering of every sort. It has not, however, made a solemn and aggressive attempt to reach the business men of middle age and of absorbing interests. The fact is, these men are in greater need of the help of the church than any other class in the community. They are in peril of the most practical and personal materialism. They are absorbed in business. Their business demands the best energies of brain, heart, body. They are laboring for the visible and the tangible. The unseen and the eternal are not naturally and immediately present. Wealth flows in upon them; and they are in danger of either that avarice or that unwise prodigality which increasing riches may develop. Wealth flies from them; and they are in danger of either that hard and rebellious or that despairing mood which misfortune may create. The constant attrition with human life may wear them into cold and polished hardness of character. The knowledge of cunning rascalities may make them pessimists. They began business, intending to be masters of business; they retire from business as its slaves. They are inclined to know nothing, to do nothing, but business. The commercial success which at first they regarded as a means to some noble purpose, they have come to consider as an ultimate aim in itself.

Such is the condition of thousands of men in the offices and stores of the cities. What can the church do for them? They are not remote from, or alien to, the church. Not a few are members of the church; many occupy their pews, with their families, on the Sabbath. They are not specially troubled with difficulties as to doctrine. They believe the Bible, respect the church, and keep the Sabbath. In answer to the question of the duty of the church, I say : —

The church should not denounce money or money-making. The church should rejoice in all the money which its members either have or gain. The church wants money, must have it. The great need of the church is men who will make money for its missionary work. The church and the ministry should discriminate, as did Christ and Paul, between money and the love of money, between riches and the trust in riches. It is not money, but the *love* of money, which is the root of all evil; it is not the riches, but the *trust* in them, which keeps us from entering heaven. Let the minister pray that his parishioners may make money; let him also pray that they may be kept from the love of money.

It is also evident that neither the church nor the ministry can serve business men by courses of sermons or addresses upon methods of business. The counting-room can teach the pulpit far better upon this theme than the pulpit the counting-room. Sermons on speculation — speculation in stocks or wheat or pork, speculations of any kind — are as valuable, and only as valuable, as Saint Anthony's sermon to the fishes. In many cases, too, they are contrary to that wise remark which Dr. Bellamy used to make to his students as to preaching : " Don't raise the Devil, young gentlemen, unless you can lay him." Many ministers cannot lay the devils which their sermons on speculation are liable to raise.

Turning to the positive side, I venture to suggest three methods that may be of worth :

Spiritual preaching. The most worldly man prefers spiritual preaching to worldly preaching. The merchant absorbed in business is sick at heart Sunday morning when his business, to which he thought he bade good-by at five o'clock the night before, again appeals to his ears in his pastor's sermon. He may rightfully claim in such an instance that his minister is robbing him of a part of his Sabbath *rest.* Ministers labor under a lamentable error when they think that college professors of natural history or of geology or of political economy want to hear sermons on Darwinism, or on the consistency of Evolution with the first chapters of Genesis, or on anarchism. The error is no less lamentable when ministers think that manufacturers and merchants, bankers and lawyers, want to be preached to as manufacturers and as merchants, as bankers and as lawyers. They want to be treated as men, — as men who have souls, as men who are tempted, as men who want all the help possible to resist temptation and to win noblest characters.

Preaching, therefore, being spiritual, should
follow the fundamental lines of thought, doctrine, teaching.   It should embrace the great
themes : sin in all forms — the self-deception
of the sinner, its self-perpetuating power, the
moral disintegration of the soul — in which
it has special allurement or power over the
business man ; God in all those qualities
and elements in which He is made known ;
human responsibility, for one's self and for
one's fellows.   But I know whereof I speak
when I affirm that the more closely the minister can centre his preaching in Christ, the
more thoroughly he will please the un-Christian as well as the Christian business men of
his congregation.   No other theme has such
power ; no other theme has such variety ; no
other theme has sources of such satisfaction.
A great court preacher, preaching before the
Queen of England, chose as his subject :
"Religion in common life."   The sermon became a favorite of Queen Victoria.   Let the
minister of the most worldly congregation select the most spiritual of subjects, — Christ

himself, — and he will not only do the most good, but also give the greatest satisfaction.

I would also beg to suggest that ministers should not fail to come into the closest personal relationship with the business men to whom they preach. It were well if ministers were even more anxious to call on the men of their churches at their places of business than on the women in their homes. If a minister is at all worthy of being known, the bank presidents and the plumbers, the lawyers and the carpenters, want to know him. The pastor should get down *close* to the hearts of the rich as well as of the poor men of his church. Not in gushing, not in the manner of the cloth, not in either fawning or patronage, but in simple and true manliness, let him know, and be known by, the busy business men. Let the men know his life as well as hear his truth.

CHAPTER VII.

FROM THE BUSINESS POINT OF VIEW.

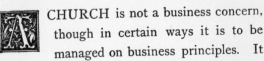 CHURCH is not a business concern, though in certain ways it is to be managed on business principles. It is not a business concern, for its purpose is not to see how it can get the most money or hire the cheapest help. Its purpose is not to save money or to secure the largest surplus. Its purpose is not to make its income equal to its expenses. The pecuniary motives of the business concern have no place as aims in the church. For the church is a spiritual institution. Its purpose is moral, ethical, Christian. Its purpose is to continue the work begun by Christ, to turn men from sin to righteousness. Its purpose relates to human character. And yet the church has a financial side. Though it is not a business institution,

it is in certain respects to be managed in a business way. Though its purpose is not to make income equal expense, yet in every church income should equal expense. The general principles of economy, efficiency, and honesty prevailing in successful business should prevail in the management of the church. In securing such principles, it seems wise for Christian business men to be the leaders in its financial interests. With their Christianity, they will manage affairs as if the church were a church; with their mercantile methods, they will make the management economical and efficient.

It is not wise usually, it seems to me, for ministers to take an active interest in the pecuniary affairs of their churches. In some cases it seems necessary for ministers to have an important part in this work. In many small churches the deacons and elders leave the pecuniary affairs of the church, as they do the spiritual, to the pastor. They ought not so to be remiss in their duty; the minister ought to cause them to take up this task belonging to them, and the doing of it would be found to be a means of grace. But in many large churches, of course, the minister not only has no need of being especially concerned in these financial matters, but also he ought not to be so concerned. Men are in the church with greater ability than his for such administration. A former pastor of one of the principal churches in New York City said to me that about one half of his time was taken up with the pecuniary affairs of the parish. His ministry was not successful, and it is not a surprise that it was a failure. Time and strength devoted to financial administration were time and strength subtracted from spiritual efficiency.

The minister, though having no active part in the financial management of his parish, should yet be deeply interested in that management; for the success or failure of his ministry may in a large degree be dependent upon the success or failure of the financial execution. He should also look upon the failure or success of the financial management of the church as a symptom of the interest or lack of interest in his work. It is to be said, however, that even business men do not employ in the management of their churches the same wisdom which they employ in the management of their own mercantile interests. A prominent church in a university town, in its love for its departing pastors, borrowed upon one occasion five thousand dollars and upon another occasion ten thousand dollars as a farewell gift. It is not wise to put a mortgage upon your principal property for the sake of making a large present to a friend. A church in New York City some years ago, out of love also for its pastor, presented him with a sum of money to meet the expenses of a trip to Europe. This sum was not the result of gifts, but was raised through a mortgage upon the church edifice. Certainly such methods are not the methods that men employ in business. The church has its financial side, and its financial interests should be administered with efficiency, economy, and honesty; and it will usually be found that the business men in a church are the best fitted thus to administer.

It is frequently said that churches are too expensive ; that the cost of being a member of a respectable church is so great that many respectable people are kept from affiliating themselves with such a congregation. It is complained that pew rentals are too high ; or if the pew rentals are not too high, that the demands for missions and missionary work are too frequent and too heavy. In some churches a basis for the charge may exist. But the reason of the complaint lies quite as much in the fault of the one complaining as in the churches themselves. In all churches are pews of which the rental is so cheap that no person earning ordinary wages should hesitate to hire them. The rental of a single pew in some churches for a year amounts to several hundred dollars. But such pews are very few, and are taken by those who are presumed to be able to pay the thousands. But even in such churches the majority of the pews can be had for a few score of dollars ; and a large number of them can be had so cheap that a single sitting costs its occupant only a few cents each week.

The charge of the too great expensiveness of churches is of course to be viewed in relation to what one receives for the expense. One receives from this financial relation to his church more than first thought might suggest. He receives the right to his sitting for two services each Sabbath. He also has a special right to all the meetings of the church of prayer, of social intercourse, of musical and literary culture. In relation to what he receives, the cost is very small.

The chief element in the cost of the administration of churches is, of course, the salary of the pastor. The salaries of a few pastors in this country are large, but of only a few. The number even of pastors having more than four thousand dollars each year is not large. In one sense a minister should receive exactly what he earns; his wages should be determined by those same laws of political economy that determine the wages of any wage-earner. In another sense he cannot receive too much. What does the minister give to his church? He does not give his brain merely, he does not give his physical strength only, — gifts which most men bring to their work ; but he also gives his heart, himself, his all. The relation between a minister and his church is more akin to that between a husband and wife than to the relation between employee and employer. A church, therefore, in one sense should not look upon their minister as a hired servant, but as one to whom, in return for his great gifts to them, they are to give all that he is able to receive. I take it that this is the relation existing between Mr. Spurgeon and the church of which he is pastor. A prominent officer of that church told me that Mr. Spurgeon was usually supposed to receive five thousand dollars a year, but that he drew whatever he wished. The church trusted him, and he trusted the church. With certain ministers this would not be possible; for, as was remarked of a prominent minister in an American city, "he would," said the treasurer of this church, "break the Bank of England."

But the charge of expensiveness of the churches is not based simply upon the parochial item, but also upon the demands for what is usually termed benevolence. The contribution box is looked upon as the symbol of this exhausting process. The notice from the pulpit for the collection is regarded as a thief regards arrest. In this same line of expensiveness, also, the pastor is supposed to be, through his personal endeavors, an especial factor. With the subscription paper in hand he goes to individuals in office and home, asking for money either for building a new chapel in the city, or to endow a college in Dakota, or to raise a testimonial fund for a retiring deacon, or to increase the annual offering for the cause of foreign or home missions.

Of such endeavors for benevolence, it seems to me that many people have a false and wrong idea. As a rule, people are not to be urged to give. As a rule, people do desire information as to Christian work. They are willing that such opportunities of Christian service should be pointed out to them; and when such information has been given and such opportunities have been pointed out, the time has come for their action. The minister has done his whole duty in giving the information, in indicating the opportunity. The subsequent action belongs to his people; and their doing, or failing to do, their duty is a question for themselves as servants of the Most High. People should constantly have placed before them opportunities for Christian giving and for Christian service. Such opportunities it would be difficult to present too frequently. But the minister should refrain from either speaking or acting in such a way as to give the impression of undue urgency. It also seems to me that it is well for a minister to refrain from soliciting personally contributions for Christian work. The temptations to such solicitation are frequently very strong. Some pastors have much success in such endeavors. A prominent minister of the Presbyterian Church himself raises the debt which afflicts the parish, or secures the money for a new organ. But, on the whole, it would be wiser for him to have a great interest in any such attempt, — to be, if one chooses, the heart of it, or even the heart and the brain of it, but not either the hands or the feet. Serving thus personally, he is in peril of lessening his spiritual influence over the character of his parishioners, for the sake of a financial gain. Such a peril he should never be willing to run. To his pastor a parishioner may not infrequently be inclined to give a larger subscription than he feels he ought. Such a subscription is far from being a means of grace to the subscriber. In general, more money will be given by a church for benevolent work if the pastor does not take a personal concern in its solicitation.

In the business management of the church, as in business management of every sort, great advantage is to be found in frequent and frank conference of officers and pastor.

If the pastor is inclined to emphasize too strongly the pecuniary side of his work, the officers should very plainly tell him his mistake, and he should be willing to bear the criticism and correct the fault. If the pastor sees in the church elements or conditions which he believes are antagonistic to its spiritual or other interests, he likewise should be very free to communicate his impressions to the officers ; and they also should bear with Christian charity the criticism, and endeavor to remedy the fault thus indicated. Church quarrels usually begin in a lack of free fraternal communication between the officers. Such communication should be very full and broad and intimate. It is thus that estrangements are avoided ; and with the avoidance of estrangements, ecclesiastical quarrels would also be prevented.

In the business management of a church, as well as in management of other kinds, it is important for the pastor so to bear himself towards his parishioners that he will appeal **to their highest needs.** He will approach them upon the highest planes of conduct and character. He will not allow himself to give the impression that he desires to make money out of them, or that his purpose in being pastor of a church is pecuniary. He will give the impression that he comes seeking, not theirs, but them. In this approach to men in their highest needs, he will be frank and hearty. As he will not suffer his parishioners to lose respect for him, so also he will not suffer himself to lose his self-respect. He will approach the members of his church as a Christian man having the highest aim, — to serve in the noblest ways those whose spiritual nurture is in no small degree committed to his keeping.

In this endeavor to foster the interests of his church, he will, above all else, love its members. Love is the universal solvent. If the minister fails to love, he should cease to be a minister. If he loves his church, his church will love him ; if he fails to love his church, his church also will fail to love him. His church is usually worthy of his love. If he love it, he can, it may be said, persuade it, as a church, to almost any line of ecclesiastical conduct. The history of churches shows that the churches in which the pastorates are long and successful are those in which the pastor has loved his church with a fulness of affection next to the love for wife and for child ; and the churches in which the pastorates have been short and have not succeeded, are those in which the pastor has not loved his church.

In the spirit of love, the pastor will be saved from the not uncommon fault of antagonizing the members of the church and the church itself. It is never wise to antagonize in church life. If a fundamental principle is under discussion, the minister must of course make known his opinion, and make his opinion impressive by wise means ; but he should never suffer himself to be led into an antagonistic mood over matters of trifling importance. Some ministers seem to have a peculiar facility for catching upon some snag in the current of ecclesiastical life, and there resting. The snag, to be sure, is small, but it holds them just as firmly from all advance in Christian service as if they were ashore. If a minister is to antagonize his church, let there be chosen a point worthy of antagonism. If there is to be a church "quarrel," let the "quarrel" be over some important point that is worthy of a battle. And as a rule, the minister is to bear himself above all parties; he is to mind his own business, which means that he is to do his own work and to do it well, and also not to meddle in the work of others.

Such a position, free from antagonism, may be gained by a right intellectual and moral perspective of the work of the church. In the church some work, some methods, some plans, are of prime importance; others are of secondary or third-rate importance. Let not the minister, for the sake of adopting methods that are of third-rate importance, suffer methods that are of secondary importance to fail. Let him not, for the sake of accomplishing work of secondary worth, allow work of

first-rate importance to suffer. Let his view
of truth be broad and accurate, adjusted to
the real conditions.

Furthermore, in the management of the
church, it is well for the minister to work
along long lines. Let him ever keep his end
in view. Let him know the discipline of
patience. Knowing that the end is of supreme importance, let him be willing to
change his methods, his means, his measures.
Let the principles of ministerial service be
laid broad, deep, and firm. Let the application of these principles be made in all wisdom
and charity. These principles, with such application, will eventually become realized. If,
for instance, that matter which at times dis-
tresses every minister — the introduction of
a better hymn-book into the Sabbath services
— perplexes him, let him not be in any special
hurry to change it. The time may not be
ripe. Many people do not want it. He may
give himself the reasonable assurance that
the service is not suffering serious loss by
reason of the use of the present book. Let

him, however, lay down the principle that the service of music in the church should be of the most elevated character; in due time this principle will become so prevalent among the people that they themselves will demand a change in the hymn-book. The adage, "A place for everything and everything in its place," may with a slight change be applied to time: A time for everything and everything in its time. The minister holding the supreme purpose of his ministry strongly, will, with waiting and righteous endeavor, find that purpose achieved.

And though all this be true, he should withal, in the managing of the interests of his parish, be a man of convictions. For his own sake and for the sake of his church, he should have, and also be willing to manifest, the courage of his convictions; manifesting this courage, of course, with all courtesy, and with a full regard for the convictions of his brethren, but holding his own as he holds his life.

CHAPTER VIII.

IN the working church are two agencies deserving particular mention, — the Sunday-school and the mid-week service. These agencies are related to our special subject as the means or methods through which the church labors.

The aim of the Sunday-school is the aim of the church, — the turning of men to righteousness through love for Christ. In securing this aim, it is of prime importance that the atmosphere, the tone, of the school be spiritual. The present is an age of machinery in ecclesiastical work. The peril is, therefore, that the spiritual will become eliminated from the life of the church. No display of knowledge as to Biblical cosmogony or geography or history should be permitted to impede spiritual activity. Much less should any endeavor for securing a large number of members or constancy of attendance be allowed to thwart the gaining of the ultimate end. Not a few schools seem like vast machine-shops in which processes and methods and tools are more manifest than the products, good and great as the products may be. Schools should be a garden in which the still atmosphere of love, the still shining of the sun of God's peace on the soil of human life, should each contribute to the growth and nurture of the individual Christian character.

The supreme purpose of the Sunday-school, however, is more vitally dependent upon its teacher than upon its general influence. Through the Sunday-school teacher the church works most directly and powerfully and effectively upon the individual. The opportunity that is open to the Sunday-school teacher is marvellous. No such opportunity for the influencing of the character of children is found outside the home. Most boys and girls do not gain much knowledge in the hour of the school. But the effect that a noble Christian man or woman has as the teacher of a boy or girl is a mighty factor in the moral character and life of that child. It is an influence somewhat akin to the influence that the Earl of Shaftesbury exerted upon a depraved man. "What did his Lordship say to you, that made you a reformed man?" was asked. "Oh, he didn't say much," was the reply. "He just sat down by my side and said, 'Jack, we will make a man out of you yet.'" It was the upward gravitation of Christian manhood that helped Jack. Such celestial attractions belong to the character of the Sunday-school teacher.

The most important element of the Christian character of the Sunday-school teacher as related to the character of the scholar, is his love for the scholar. No amount of Biblical knowledge, indeed, no degree of intellectual skill in presenting the truth, can supply the lack of personal affection. If a teacher loves, his intellectual qualifications will become the more useful. This love cannot be simulated. Young human nature detects the counterfeit as quickly as the bank balances the depraved coin. The teacher is to be willing to sacrifice himself for his class. He is to respect its members. He is to have a regard for them, not in the mass, but as individuals. "He calleth his own sheep by name." Having a love for each, he will also have a knowledge of each, in the home and the school, in the trials and the joys, in the past and the hopes of each. Furthermore, the teacher bearing this love to his pupils is to feel free to talk with each pupil as to his personal character. The teacher is to be the pastor of the class ; he is to be the shepherd of this little flock. He is to be the great aid of the parent in training each boy or each girl into Christian manhood or womanhood. It would be well if the teacher should be not less of a teacher but more of a pastor, and if each teacher should recognize himself as the pastor of the class.

To the giving of such personal influence

most members of the Sunday-school easily
offer themselves by reason of their age. A
large proportion of the Sunday-school consists of young people. It is to the young
people that we are to look for the beginning
of the Christian life. In a recent meeting at
St. Paul, a distinguished evangelist asked for
the age of the conversion of those who were
in the audience. The audience numbered
about twelve hundred people. He first asked
for those who became Christians after the age
of fifty to rise, and one arose. He asked next
for those who became Christians between the
ages of forty and fifty to rise, and one rose.
Then he asked in turn for those to rise who
became Christians between thirty and forty,
and twenty-one rose ; for those between
twenty-five and thirty, and thirty-eight rose ;
for those between twenty and twenty-five,
and one hundred rose ; for those who became
Christians before twenty years of age, and six
hundred rose. The larger share of the members of the school consists of those who are
below the age of twenty. It is the age of con-

version. It is the period when the teacher's love and words have the strongest influence in leading boys and girls into the acceptance and confession of Christ.

In the Sunday-school the working church works in and through its teacher. The remark of Garfield that the best college for him was a log, at one end of which sat President Hopkins and at the other James A. Garfield, is quite as true of spiritual discipline as of intellectual. The best church is that which has the best Sunday-school, and the best Sunday-school is that which has the best teacher.

A second agency which the working church employs in its administration is the mid-week service.

It has been said, by the best of recent English historians, that the England of the Puritan was a nation of a book, and that book was the Bible. It may likewise be said that the mid-week service of the church is becoming the study of a book, and that book is the Bible. The prayer and conference meeting is undergoing a change, not of purpose, but of method. This meeting of a former generation partook of the character of a lecture conducted by the pastor, deacons, and elders. Undoubtedly it had many advantages. If it were dull, as it not infrequently was to the younger attendants, it certainly was edifying in Christian character to the more mature. Within the memory of many young Christians, this type has become comparatively extinct. It has been followed by a meeting of quite a different character, in which the interest and profit were measured by the number who took part. The meeting was a meeting of testimony. The minister asked not for speeches, but for talks. The briefer were the more acceptable ; and the more personal they were, the greater was their power. This form of meeting still continues. It has much to commend it. It is a most important means of Christian growth. It suggests one cause of the marvellous growth of the Methodist Church. Its principle is the central principle in the admirable Christian Endeavor movement. It is of great usefulness in leading men to the personal acceptance of Christ. It promotes the sense of personal responsibility. It is a constant and public confession of Christ. It develops the spiritual life. Its peril is the fostering of a mechanical and hollow type of piety. Its danger lies in lacking intellectual and Scriptural substance. Its weakness consists in the development of self-consciousness.

But this type of meeting is being already somewhat pushed aside by a third and in many respects a higher form. The central principle of this meeting is knowledge of the Scriptures. Its method is determined by the Bible. Its purpose is edification by the Word of God. This type of meeting is less a study of the Bible in its historical or ethical, doctrinal or theological relations, than in its practical. It seeks to know the mind of God as thus recorded upon all those subjects which relate to the upbuilding of individual character. It is a Bible reading, conducted not by the leader, but by the

whole congregation.   Various and diverse are
the measures used in conducting it.   The
subject, announced in advance, may be an-
alyzed, and different divisions assigned to
different members for treatment.   Slips, with
certain passages of Scripture indicated, may
be distributed among a dozen or more for
reading when they are asked for.   The leader
should, at all events, hold the meeting in his
own keeping, making the best of the com-
ments, yet encouraging the habit of asking
questions ; suggesting many passages of Scripture, yet encouraging in every way the habit
of independent study of the Word of God.
The mid-week service of this type is in widely
separated parts of the country becoming popular.   An eminent pastor said to me recently
that he does not care to hear the voice of the
attendants upon the prayer-meeting of his
church, except as the truth of the Bible is
indicated.   In the church of which I am the
minister, this method seems to work to the
satisfaction and profit of all.   It combines
the advantages of the two forms of meetings

to which I have alluded. It is in the best sense edifying, tending to build up the individual character in the simple truth of God. It promotes the sense of individual responsibility. It fosters constant public confession of Christ. It has warmth with light, appealing to the feelings, yet having sufficient intellectual substance and vigor. It turns the eye of the soul away from itself to the Father and Saviour. This method succeeds in avoiding stupidity and dulness; it stops the long and hopeless exhortations; it gives movement and progress.

If the prayer-meeting were more true to its name, there would be less cause for rejoicing over this evolution of the Bible meeting. But the prayer-meeting is not true to its name. It has become a " remarks " meeting, — remarks which are of some worth, but not of such a degree of worth as an hour in which a few score or a few hundred men and women of intelligence and piety assemble together, ought to offer. But the Bible meeting demands and promotes piety and intelligence, quickens the heart and the brain, and endeavors to support sound practice with sound theory and to cause sound theory to eventuate in sound practice.

The causes of this development or tendency are manifold ; but the chief cause is the same general movement which in theological seminaries results in the introduction of Biblical theology into the course of study, which in the college is demanding that the Bible be made the object of special attention, which in the Sunday-school is contributing to the enlightened as well as reverent study of the Word of God. The age is an age of inquiry. Systems of theology have use, — a use of prime importance. But this age of inquiry has gone back of theological treatises to that Book which is the fountain and source of whatever in those treatises is of enduring worth.

It may prove of aid in conducting such Bible meetings as the mid-week service to bear in mind : —

(1) That the subject considered should be

drawn immediately from life. It should possess the most interesting practical interest. The Bible fosters the choice of subjects of this character. It is concerned chiefly with human life and with God's relation to human life.

(2) That all finical and allegorical interpretations should be avoided. Sound common-sense should be predominant in all exegesis. Men of sense, Christian or un-Christian, are repelled by interpretations which lack sense.

(3) That topics chosen should be so broad as to lend themselves to easy division and to give that variety of personal reference and application which the Christian in the variety of his spiritual needs may require.

CHAPTER IX.

TREATMENT OF STRANGERS.

THE church is not primarily a social institution; it is primarily a religious institution. Yet the social relations of its members have a primary importance in the development of the church as a religious institution. The problem — simple in its terms, though far from simple in its solution — which each church has thus presented to itself, is, How can we attract strangers to our services? How can we secure their introduction to ourselves and to our work? How can we the most speedily and courteously cause them to be at home with us? In answering these questions I can hardly hope to give more than suggestions.

But before making any attempt, it may be said that those moving into a town and attending its church as strangers owe certain duties to that town and to that church as well as the town and the church to them. These duties are seldom considered. Pastors endeavor to open wide the doors of hospitality to strangers; but they are prevented from driving or pushing strangers through the portals. They exhort the older members to be cordial; but their sense of courtesy forbids their preaching to strangers upon the proper methods of accepting offers of hospitality.

It is, we doubt not, the experience of the large majority of ministers that strangers fail in their duty to the church far more lamentably than the church fails in its duty to them. In every congregation are a few who from the first morning they are shown to a pew are as ready to receive attention as the older members are prompt to bestow it. But nine tenths are far otherwise. They hold themselves aloof from the church services. They occupy the rear seats at the prayer-meeting; and before the pastor can reach the door they

are in the street. They receive a dozen calls
at their homes, but wait months before re-
turning them, even if they see fit to return
them at all. In a large Congregational church
of a large Massachusetts city two ladies made
in a month seventy-five calls upon those who
were comparative strangers. Of these seventy-
five calls only one received its fitting and
courteous acknowledgment. The wife of the
pastor of a church less than a thousand miles
from Boston has a rule of calling upon all
new people coming into the congregation.
The proportion of those who return her calls
is about one to five. In that respect of which
strangers usually complain bitterly of a church,
they are themselves most derelict. Strangers
are also, as a body, negligent in contributing
to the financial support of a church as soon
as they have decided to make it their religious home. The writer knows of a lady who
remarked, after attending a church for a year,
that she was ashamed to be seen there longer
without renting a seat. She felt as she ought
to feel, — that as soon as possible after her en-

trance she should hire a seat and pay for it. Many strangers are also inclined not to be faithful in contributing to the directly religious welfare of the church. They do not let their light shine in the meetings of devotion as early as they ought. For Christian modesty, humility, and the passive virtues we have great reverence ; but they are ever to be distinguished from positive indifference or unassuming selfishness.

What, then, is the duty of strangers to the church which is so seldom paid ? The duty is the very simple one of making themselves known ; of holding themselves ready to receive attentions from the older members ; of declaring, in forms either direct or indirect, their desire to co-operate in the work of the church. They should come towards the church, not perhaps half-way in accepting its hospitalities, but at least a quarter way. They should not only manifest their willingness to receive the social courtesies of the members, but also their hearty purpose and wish to return all such courtesies in fitting ways. They should let their voice be heard in the service of song and of prayer. They should let the influence of their dollars be felt in the revenue of the parish and in the benevolent offerings. They should give people a chance to shake their hand. And all this they should do at the earliest possible day after making their home in the neighborhood of the church.

In the swiftly changing communities of our cities the new members of any congregation soon find themselves the old members. Within a decade one half of the ordinary congregation of the cities changes, and at the close of a period of twenty-five years hardly one member in ten remains. Much sooner, therefore, than they would think, have the strangers become the established residents. Upon them, therefore, at an early day devolves the duty of showing those same rites of hospitality which were shown to them. They ought to forget, as soon as may be, that they are new members, and so become an integral part of the essential and aggressive forces of the church.

For its social work the church should be furnished with a body of ushers, and also with a reception committee. The work of these gentlemen is limited to the more public services. It should, however, include the larger week-day prayer-meetings as well as the services of Sunday. The reception committee should remain in or near the vestibule of the church at each public service to extend a greeting to strangers. Its members should know the congregation so well that they can at once detect those who are " new-comers." The welcome thus given should be hospitable, courteous, neither effusive nor indifferent. It should, by both words and manner, indicate the heartiness of the greeting of those who are personal friends in Christ, even if they are not in each other. The member of the reception committee who thus welcomes them should at once say to the usher that the gentleman or lady is a stranger and would be glad to be shown to a seat. This semi-introduction may give the usher a sufficient occasion to speak a word of greeting. But in the coming of many strangers into a large congregation, any conversation is necessarily brief and fragmentary. It is not, therefore, unfitting for the usher to adopt some more satisfactory method for extending the courtesy of the church. I know of at least one church in which a body of polite and faithful ushers has found the following method of much worth. Each usher has a small card, on one side of which is printed this : —

"If you are a stranger in this church it would give me pleasure to see you at the close of the service and to introduce you to our pastor and other members."

This simple invitation is signed by the name of the usher. On the obverse side is a blank space for the name and address of the one who receives the card. This method has various advantages. It gives the stranger an opportunity for knowing somewhat of the service of the church before revealing his identity. He need not be hurried against his will into taking up a connection which he may regret. It is not too effusive. It is yet sufficiently aggressive in the offers of hospitality. It invites accuracy in identifying each person. It puts each stranger in the line of the personal life and work of the church. In the execution of this plan the number of ushers must be large, and they should be aided by the reception committee and by others who may be blessed with social gifts. Emphasis should also be constantly laid by the pastor upon the duty of all pew-holders speaking to strangers whom they may meet. It may also be noted that it is well to pursue a similar method in the case of large prayer-meetings. Along this line it may be suggested that the pastor at the close of the prayer-meeting should make his way to the door through which the people pass, and should give to each one a hearty greeting. I know of able ministers who indicate their hospitality in a like way at the close of the Sabbath morning service. Selecting the aisle which is the least filled, they rush to the door of exit. I confess that such a procedure under the circumstances seems to me to be lacking in dignity. It is far better for the ushers to meet strangers at the close of the service, and to escort them to the pastor, who remains near the stairway to the pulpit.

As soon as one indicates his desire to feel at home in a church, the people of that church should extend to him the ordinary courtesy through calling at his home. Every church should have its committee upon strangers, but no church should demand that this committee have all the pleasure of first knowing these strangers. The members of this committee should indeed call at the home of strangers, but they should also make these strangers known to those of the church who live in the same neighborhood into which they have moved. In a large church it is quite impossible for any one person to know more than a small proportion of all the members. Acquaintance, therefore, in the same neighborhood should be specially fostered. The chairman of the committee on strangers, therefore, at once on knowing that a family in a neighborhood desires to become associated with the church, should communicate the fact to the older members residing in the same neighborhood, and ask them to call and to know the new residents. This method tends to do away with a mere formality of church acquaintance. It tends to found this acquaintance upon genuinely social as well as ecclesiastical considerations. It makes acquaintance easy because natural. It is economical in labor and time. It is simple ; it adopts the principle of the division of labor, and wherever it has been wisely applied it has proved of much worth.

The traditional "social" should not be slighted in the organized endeavor of the church. But the "social" should always be sociable. If it is cold in its atmosphere and filled with unnecessary formalities, it is a dull, gloomy, distressing occasion. The hour should not be so filled with music and readings and addresses as to leave no time for conversation, and yet the hour should not be so devoid of such pleasures as to seem vacant and bare. The socials should also recognize the fact that it is much easier to be sociable over a cup of coffee!

It remains to be added that as the pastor succeeds in getting strangers at work in the church, they cease to be strangers. The work identifies them with the church. Work promotes knowledge of, and love for, the church. The sooner the pastor is able to assign some individual Christian duty to each new member, the sooner he may throw aside all responsibility as to mere social acquaintance. Work for Christ and His church makes all one. Let the church hold itself as a spiritual institution, using social courtesies as agencies in its spiritual development. It is also true that the use of social courtesies as means renders them more social and more courteous than if they are regarded as ends.

CHAPTER X.

THE UNCHURCHED.

CLUSTERING about many churches, be they in the city or in the country, is a population as remote from the church in sentiment as it may be near to it in space. As to the duty of the church to endeavor to reach these people there is no question. The question is as to the method of reaching those who are thus unchurched. I answer, first, that a systematic religious census should be made of all the families of each city, town, and parish. The church census is not designed as a substitute for spiritual power. Its express purpose is to facilitate and to make more effective the work of the Holy Ghost. Nor is its aim the annulling of the religious duties of the members of a church. It proposes to increase these duties and to add to their obligation. The Massachusetts pastor was as right in his logic as he was wrong in his piety in saying that he did not desire his church to make this canvass, since it would give the members too much to do !

The church census is simply a voyage of discovery to learn who are outside of direct religious influences, for the purpose of drawing those thus found within the circle of these influences. It is a movement preliminary to the wise presentation of the ordinances of the church to those not receiving them. The motive is spiritual, the method simple, and the means accessible.

The present conditions of social and religious life emphasize the need of a canvass of this character in each town. The inclination of non-attendance at church is strong. The causes of this inclination may be open to debate ; the fact is generally acknowledged. Population circulates rapidly. Families have no permanent abiding-place. The American home, like that of George Eliot in her last years, is on wheels. The increasing custom of renting houses invites this constant rotation. Furthermore, the drift of population from rural districts to metropolitan centres is great, — hardly less great in the West than in the East.

The church census is therefore needed. For the constant or irregular migration from town to town loosens the religious ties of the ordinary home. Without special desire of availing itself of the privileges of the church, the family fails to take up a connection with the church in the new neighborhood. It simply falls out of all ecclesiastical relationship. This condition every minister knows is not infrequent. The canvass reveals families of this nature. It so makes them known that the church not only can open its doors to them, but even invite them to enter. The urban movement of population works similar effects. Many persons from country homes are inclined to feel that they are not wanted in the city churches. The feeling is, I believe, not accordant with the facts, yet it is more or less sincere. The religious census of a city discovers not a few homes, whose members are church-members, in which this sentiment prevails. The knowledge of the fact prompts to urgency in the extending of the courtesies of the church.

We present on page 113 a series of questions which should be asked of each family of a town, through a personal canvass. This form has also been employed in a census.

The census represents the proper attitude of the churches toward those who are inclined to neglect their services. This attitude should be that of hearty invitation. The church, like Christ, is sent to find the *lost* sheep. It is not merely to invite, it is also to go out into the highways and the byways and compel, them to come in. The minister who, when asked what he was doing to reach people, replied, "Opening the doors of the church Sunday morning," had failed to grasp the central truth of Christianity. By its very constitution the church cannot be anything else than missionary. This attitude of the churches is at the present time of special

DATE...*NO*..............

No...............*Street*...................................

Name...

Members of.................. ....

Attendance or Preference.............................

Members elsewhere or letter..........................

No. in family...................*Under 21 years*..............

No. who attend S. S............*Where*....................

Servants..

Boarders..

Willing to teach in S. S...................................

Have you a Bible ?..

Remarks...

....

....

☞ Will the pastor to whom this is sent keep this slip for future reference and use?

8

importance. For communities both change and increase rapidly in population. In twenty-five years the constituency of many urban and suburban churches undergoes a complete revolution. In these swift changes many families fail to form any relation, other than the slightest, with a church. If they know the church, the church, under ordinary conditions, fails to know them. A minister of a church in a city, either large or small, or in a village, cannot learn the ecclesiastical preferences of families that are more or less peripatetic. But such families should be reached ; if not reached, they fail to receive the gospel quite as much as the heathen.

But this canvass is of greatest worth in forming a basis of more definite and more aggressive Christian work. The canvass reveals those who are unchurched ; the minister and congregation should at once endeavor to gather them into the church. When the census makes known " backsliders," efforts should at once be made to reclaim them. When the census discovers children who are members of no Sunday-school, Sunday-school committees should at once be sent to bring them into classes. If the church has no room for these new-comers, room should in some way be made. The privileges of the house of God should be denied to no soul by reason of lack of square feet of flooring. If one church cannot give them room, another may be able. Certainly under *some* ecclesiastical roof-tree they should find a Christian church-home.

The endeavor to reach the unchurched should not simply be systematic, it should also be constant. Systematic visitation should be continued, not for six months, but for years. Constant pressure is more effective for the proposed purpose than heavy periodical pressure. Furthermore, both the church and the minister should strive to retain even the slightest ties which may connect a family with the church. The service at a wedding or a funeral may be the small cord which may in years grow into the cable uniting the individual family to the church-home.

In many instances, instead of the man
coming to the church, the church must go to
the man. The church is apostolic, missionary. In this aggressive endeavor no methods
are more worthy of attention than those of
Mr. McAll in Paris.

For several years the churches and ministers of the United States have been talking
as to means and measures for reaching the
unchurched of the large cities. The general
difficulty with many means and measures
proposed is the difficulty of most patents, —
complication ; the machinery is too elabo-
rate. The methods of Mr. McAll represent
the simplicity of spiritual genius and the
genius of simplicity.

The first point relates to a place of meeting. The stations of the McAll Mission are
rooms, seating from one hundred and fifty to
three hundred persons, plainly furnished, yet
attractive, with chairs and pictures, on the
ground floor, and usually in places where
people " most do congregate." To reach the
masses, one must go where the masses are.

We must get as close to them as we can. It is not necessary to build a church edifice. A simple, attractive room, on the ground floor, brilliantly lighted at night, is far more effective than a building which in form and structure proclaims its religious purpose. To effect this purpose of gathering in all classes, the place of meeting must be immediately off the street. Mr. McAll would never have achieved his present success had he obliged Frenchmen to climb a flight of stairs to attend his services. We cannot evangelize Boston, or New York, or Chicago on the second floor. In every way should the approach to the room in which these evangelistic services are held be made easy and attractive. Placard and gas should draw and hold the attention. The surroundings should be inviting to the evening stroller. A word of welcome should await him at the threshold, and be continued and emphasized with a warm grasp of the hand within the doors.

A second point as important as the location and attractiveness of the place of meet-

ing relates to the character of the meeting.
The service, first of all, should be interesting.
If it is dull or stupid, it is a failure for its immediate aim.   It is impossible to hold the
unconverted masses without interesting them.
In gaining this purpose, the power of song
has, in France, proved most effective.   The
Moody and Sankey songs are translated and
sung quite as much in Paris as in New York.
The wanderers on the streets at night can
be thus attracted.   These songs are open to
criticism on grounds of reverence and truthfulness as well as of æsthetics.   But for their
purpose of drawing and holding the masses,
they are unequalled.   Scores of people will
come off the street to sing,

"The half was never told,"

who would turn away from the most eloquent
sermon.

But a meeting at a McAll station is incom-
plete without an address.   This address is
usually a direct, personal, warm, wise appeal.
I have seen scores of the blue-jacketed work-

men of Paris listening to such appeals. Some
were listless, more were touched in heart,
most were interested. Will not the laborers
of Boston, New York, and Chicago likewise
listen ? The masses of the American people
seem to me less hungry for the gospel than
the masses of the French people; but I am
constrained to believe that under proper conditions scores, if not hundreds, could be
gathered night by night into little mission
rooms in our great cities, — scores who now
do not enter a church once a year.

Work of this character demands a man,
and demands money. It requires wisdom,
faith, hope, tact, patience, and, above all else,
a love for perishing souls and a love for
Christ who died to save them. But is it not
a method of work the success of which in
the new republic of the Old World gives a
promise of its success in the old republic of
the New World ? Is not God able to do,
through us, for American cities what He is
doing through an English Congregational minister for Paris and other French cities ?

If the individual church would do its duty
to those who live in its immediate vicinity,
and who neglect all religious services, it were
well. Yet even such faithfulness would not
effect results equal to the general needs. For
beyond the immediate vicinity of the churches, in parts of the cities whence churches
have withdrawn, are thousands of people who
are without the help which the church should
be able and willing to offer. In each country
district, too, miles away from any church, are
many families, who are more bereft of the privileges of the church than the Fiji Islanders.
Many churches are devoting every energy to
keeping themselves alive. They feel unable
to be aggressive in either personal or pecuniary effort. They yield to the up-town pressure of the tide of the better class of people.
They seek what is recognized as a more
desirable constituency. They are not worthy
of blame only, since their mistake is quite as
much one of method as of motive ; but the
church, however, should know that it can
maintain its integrity only by bringing into

its life as constant factors those who dwell about its edifice. For the purpose of bringing these persons into the church, every means of personal visitation and attractiveness in service should be employed.

For the purpose, however, of reaching the non-churchgoing population, the union of churches in aggressive endeavor may prove of much worth. The organic union of all denominations of Protestants is a hope born of the unreasoning heart of the religious enthusiast. Organic union is not possible, and if it were possible, is not to be desired. And if organic union were once formed, it is more than probable that the union thus formed would for religious efficiency become disunion. But union for Christian work is possible at the present time, and is more to be desired than any other practical method of evangelization. It is thus that neighborhoods having too few churches may be supplied with religious privileges. It is thus that neighborhoods having too many churches may spend their superfluous strength in destitute districts.   It is thus that the evils of an over-multiplication of churches may be avoided, and religion instead of rivalries promoted.

The history of Christianity since the apostolic age, when there were Cephasites, Apollosites, Paulists, and Christians, has been the history of ecclesiastical divisions.   The list of these divided members of the one body of our Lord is to-day longer than ever.   The pastor has been too eager to build up his individual church, and not sufficiently eager to build up the whole church of his order ; and the whole church of all orders has suffered.   The whole church of one order has been too solicitous to build up itself, and not sufficiently solicitous to build up the whole church of all orders ; the church universal has suffered.[1]   The time has now come when the broadest and highest motives should have a controlling influence.   Denominational methods have proved

[1] " The Catholic religion respects masses of men, and ages.   It is in harmony with Nature, which loves the race and ruins the individual.   The Protestant has his pew, which of course is the first step to a church for every individual citizen, a church apiece." — *Journal of R. W. Emerson, Cabot's Memoir*, p. 472.

insufficient. Interdenominational methods of work are not practicable. Undenominational methods are at once practicable, desirable, and full of promise. With a basis as broad and strong as the love for God and man, let all the churches unite in the aggressive warfare against the world, the flesh, and the devil. With a doctrinal union as firm and elastic as the Apostles' creed, let all those confessing the one Name in which alone there is salvation, become one in purpose, methods, and movement. Let co-operation take the place of competition, and diversity be substituted for division.

The religious census is the beginning of this advance. The second step is the systematic visitation and personal invitation to participate in the work and worship of the church. Personal conversation upon the most personal, which is also the most important, of subjects should become usual. Those classes now neglecting and neglected by the church may thus be won into close and helpful fellowship. Let the churches unite in caring for districts in our own land that are now more heathen than Japan.

Such a united movement would be most useful in calming the ruffled waters which are so stirred up by socialistic agitations. By hanging bomb-throwers, the law cannot put out the fires hissing in the furnace of public discontent. The gospel alone can cure socialism and anarchy; and the gospel must cure socialism and anarchy, or they will not be cured. The divine love as the divine law for human acceptance, and the divine love as the divine law for human obedience, must become supreme. The Church, the one Church of the one Christ, having one body though many members, and each member adjusted to every other, should, in love for Him and love for man, give itself, in a Christlike spirit and according to wise methods, to these Gentiles of its own Judæa.

NOTE. — In answer to the question " What can the ordinary church do to reach the masses? " the Rev. Dr. D. A. Reed (Proceedings of the Second Convention of Christian Workers in the United States and Canada, Sept. 21–28, 1887, p. 32) has suggested these methods : —

" In concluding, let me summarize : ' What can the ordinary church do to reach the masses ? '

" (1) Let the services of the church be simple, pleasing, and attractive.

" (2) Have special evangelistic services in the evening, with good music.

" (3) Have a well-manned Sunday-school, with building suitable for class-rooms for a large number of adult classes ; also where classes can meet during the week for literary and social purposes.

" (4) Have educational classes, and lectures on certain evenings, on the great burning questions of the day, by live, earnest men.

" (5) Where a church numbers over three hundred, have two pastors, or a pastor and a trained assistant, devoting his whole time to the work, under the direction of the pastor or supplementing him.

" (6) Make much of personal work, the efforts of individuals whose hearts are full of love for souls. Have a band of men and women trained in the Bible, who shall know how to use it and love to use it, ready to work in all meetings of an evangelistic character in the inquiry-room, ready to go and see individuals and converse with them about their spiritual needs, wise to win souls.

" (7) Have the parish districted, and find out where the people attend church, if possible ; and if they do not attend, go for them and invite them, not once but many times.

" (8) Have branch chapels or cottage prayer-meetings, or both, in the districts where fewest people attend church. They will often go into these places when they will not go into the church.

" (9) Have a sufficient number of visitors for each district, so that too many families will not be given to any one.

" (10) Have classes into which those who are converted can enter and be instructed in the great doctrines of Christianity, and taught how to study the Bible with profit and pleasure, and how to engage in some form of Christian work.

" (11) Set the converts to work, watching, directing, encouraging them until they get to love it and consecrate themselves to it. Show them, by the teaching and example of pastor and older Christians, that the great aim of the church is to bear true witness to the gospel of Jesus Christ and save men. Show each Christian that he or she has a personal work to do with persons ; that money and prayers are not sufficient; that sympathy and love and personal solicitude for the comfort and salvation of men are what the masses need.

"(12) Money, brains, consecration, and the aid of the Holy Spirit will enable any ordinary church to win the masses."

CHAPTER XI.

BENEVOLENCE.

CERTAIN principles every pastor may and should impress upon his church.

(1) All property should be consecrated to God. The Christian's wealth is not his ; it is Christ's, to whom he himself belongs. He is, therefore, to keep or to give, to hoard or to spend, as will result most fully in the doing of the Divine will. He may, like Deacon Safford, place a self-imposed limit on the wealth he will retain, giving away each year whatever he finds in excess. He may, like not a few, reserve ten per cent of his income for benevolence. He may give away large amounts or small, either in person or by bequest. But whatever method he adopts, the principle is to be followed that property belongs to God.

(2) The peril of great property, which is worldliness, is best avoided by great benevolence. Many members of our churches are becoming rich, and not a few very rich. The United States is to be the richest nation of history. Many men making money rapidly can keep alive their Christian faith only by giving away a certain percentage of it as rapidly as it is made. " I grow avaricious," said a prosperous banker, "if I do not give away much money." Benevolence is an ethical and Christian safeguard.

(3) Benevolence is a duty laid upon all. Churches distinguished for their generosity usually gain their eminence from the generosity of a few. An offering recently made in a Presbyterian church of New York amounted to some fourteen thousand dollars. It was heralded as a munificent contribution ; but in it was one check for ten thousand dollars, and the larger part of the balance was given by two or three men. I have been told of a contribution of sixteen thousand dollars, of which fifteen thousand dollars were given by three

contributors. Each should not only give, but each should give in proportion to his means.

(4) The larger one's property or income, the larger should be the percentage of his benevolence. The tithe represents a great fundamental principle. But one hundred dollars from an income of a thousand is, relatively to the needs of a home, a much larger sum than a thousand dollars drawn from an income of ten thousand. The thousand dollars may hardly more than suffice to buy necessaries; the ten thousand, after supplying the common wants, leaves a large balance for permanent investment. On the whole, rich men are relatively less generous than poor men.

(5) The just demands of benevolence are to be recognized as imperative. What do they not include? Home missions and foreign, charitable organizations of every sort, philanthropic movements, the endowment of colleges and schools and seminaries, and every endeavor looking to the redemption of the world from sin and unto Christ, are within the horizon of these just demands. Almost

daily comes some appeal to the desk from which this chapter was written. Each appeal is worthy. By itself each demand seems to deserve prompt and generous response. Every secretary of every mission board hourly hears the cry for help. To refuse to hear the cry always means retrenchment of the work, frequently retreat, and sometimes absolute defeat. Despite their great generosity, most churches and most Christians have no conception of either the duty or the joy of giving money to Christ's work in the world.

(6) Benevolence should not be subject to impulse, but the result of wise deliberation upon the needs of Christian work. Offerings should not be proportioned to the interest which a speaker for a cause may or may not awaken; they should not be dependent upon a rainy Sunday or upon personal presence in a service in which the contribution box is passed. Their amount should be adjusted to income and to property on the one side, and to the demands of the work on the other. They

should be systematic, — systematic as to time, as to amount, as to distribution. They should be the subject of premeditation, and in many instances of pledge in advance. The objection, so often made, to pledging an offering of a certain sum, since the amount of future income is an uncertain quality, is not candid. Pledges made toward the benevolences of a church are usually so made that to cancel them is easy. Furthermore, the objection is so based as to lose all definitive force. Every family lives in a certain recognized way, though its future income is unknown.

For this general work of the church the system of annual pledges and weekly gifts is the best. The system is an education in benevolence. It is an education in the feeling of benevolence, but it is also an education in the principle of benevolence. It tends to make giving constant and wise. It emphasizes the duty. Unless one is trained, he seldom gives according to his ability. The largest givers, proportionally to their means, are found among those who have been thus educated in and from youth. This system teaches children as well as men. It attracts and retains the pennies and five-cent pieces. The constant regularity develops the generous impulses and motives.

Akin to this advantage of education is a second which the system offers. It tends to change benevolent offerings from being regarded as acts of grace to being regarded as acts of regular church administration. It lessens the inclination to judge benevolence as a work of supererogation. This inclination is strong. Many nominal Christians look on the field of foreign and home missions as one to which they bear no relation. If they aid in maintaining missions, the assistance is considered as a favor bestowed and not as a duty done. They do not look on the American Board as a society doing *their* work in China and Africa. They do not regard the Home Missionary Society as *their* representative in the churches of Minnesota and Missouri and Texas. They do not consider the American Missionary Association as *their* teacher and preacher to the American black man and red man. This, however, is precisely the fact. These and all other societies are simply the churches organized and working for certain ends. If this work is at all a duty, the support of it is not an act of grace, but of duty. The regular giving tends to foster this just estimate of it.

The system of weekly offerings, furthermore, encourages all to benevolence. It encourages specially those whose gifts must be small. One easily gives twenty-five cents a week who would not feel able to pledge twelve dollars a year. It is easier to give a small sum regularly than a large sum, in the aggregate no greater, irregularly. Those who are accustomed to give nothing, through this system are usually moved to give something. Those who are accustomed to give largely are thus moved to give more largely. The man who is accustomed to give twenty-five dollars a quarter discovers that he can and ought to give more than two dollars a Sunday. Subdivision, by diminishing the amount of each gift, at once convinces those who are not wealthy that they are able to give something, and those who are wealthy that they are able to give more generously.

Following from this advantage is a fourth, which is that the amount of offerings is thus greatly increased. The statistics show that the introduction of the system usually results in a gain of from 20 to 200 per cent. Of three churches in Massachusetts one reported a gain of 300 per cent, one of between 400 and 500, and one of not less than 500, consequent upon the adoption of this method. Of this increase there is indeed abundant need, when, in a rich and generous Commonwealth like Massachusetts, each Congregational church-member gives less than five cents a day for the maintenance and extension of the church at home and abroad.

The disadvantages of the system are few and slight. The uncertainty of income, the uncertainties due to sickness and other disabilities, render it inexpedient, it is said, to pledge for a year in advance a specified weekly gift. But each person can usually be assured of a certain income. He can make his calculations upon this basis ; and if the 31st of December shows that he has been prospered more than he dared to hope, his blessing may fitly be recognized and bestowed as a thank-offering. The pledge is, indeed, not one to be kept except as one is financially able to keep it.

In the use of pledges, the apparent publicity of the system would seem objectionable. But this publicity is only apparent. At the furthest the treasurer alone knows the amount of each offering ; and usually he is ignorant, — for an account is kept, not of the names of the givers, but of certain numbers which represent the givers.

This system of weekly offerings, though so excellent, does not succeed of itself. It needs, without exception, to be *worked*. A poor system well applied may prove more effective than a good system ill applied. This method requires constant instruction and appeal.

In his own relation to the benevolence of his church, the pastor should impress himself with the duty, (1) of giving full and exact information to the members as to the condition of those missionary endeavors in which they invest ; (2) of never suffering himself to be tempted by meagre contributions into petulance or scolding ; (3) of setting a fitting example himself ; (4) of wisdom in approaching individuals as to the time, place, and amount ; (5) of the education of the young and old in generous giving ; (6) of persistence, which is only aggressive patience.

But principles even broader and more fundamental than those to which I have already alluded are to be made potent in the administration. It is hardly too much to say that money is the greatest material power in the modern world for either good or evil. " It can do," as Mr. Dombey said to Paul, — " it can do anything, almost." The expression may seem bold, yet it is true, — that the pastor should inspire his parishioners to make money for Christ. This is an age of differentiation in work. The workman who fifty years ago knew a whole trade, now knows only one branch of that trade. The editor of the old times was the printer; his hands set up and struck off the copy which the same hands had written. To-day, on a large paper, each department commands several writers. This differentiation runs through all departments of labor. It exists in Christian work. The old New England minister received a part of his salary in the farm which surrounded the parsonage. He raised the oats and hay for the horse which carried him over his parish; and potatoes and corn for the family use. To-day, in most parts, he gives himself entirely to his work as a minister, and allows his parishioners to attend to agriculture. The missionary goes to China; he goes simply as a missionary. He goes with no purpose of earning a livelihood. But he must have a livelihood. Now, with this differentiation and subdivision of labor, it becomes the duty of the home church to make money for his livelihood. In a New

England State is a farmer who has been a missionary. He has sisters in Asia who are now missionaries. He desires to aid them in their work. But he can aid them more effectively by staying at home, and on a Vermont farm coining the dollars which are devoted to the wise and effective prosecution of their distant labor. Prayers are essential, conversion is essential, personal effort is essential; but benevolence is equally essential in Christian work.

But money is not only an essential means of doing good, money is also the means of doing the *widest* good. Civilization increases the power of the dollar. "A dollar in a university," remarks Emerson, in his essay on Wealth, "is worth more than a dollar in a jail; in a temperate, schooled, law-abiding community, than in some sink of crime, where dice, knives, and arsenic are in constant play." The electric telegraph has widened the dollar's circle of influence. One can sit in his dining-room and write a message which shall, before he finishes his dinner, put bread in the mouths of starving men in China. He is feeding them just as truly as if he were in Pekin, and standing on a street corner giving away food. One can sit in his pew in a church of New York or San Francisco, of New Orleans or Minneapolis, and by his generosity dictate the removal of the barbarism, and the enlightenment by Christianity, of Asia and Africa. The forces of the air co-operate with each Christian in his continental labor of love. Puck put his girdle around the world in forty minutes. The Christian of the United States can put his girdle of consecrated gold as quickly around the globe; and wherever it touches the earth, its flashes of divine influence illuminate the night of heathendom.

At the opening of this century lived in Salem a rich merchant by the name of John Norris. Three years before the establishment of the American Board he had resolved to give a sum of money to the cause of foreign missions. To his home came, one winter night in 1806, Dr. Worcester and Dr. Spring, of Newburyport. The reverend gentlemen were endeavoring to found a theological school at Andover. After explaining their plan, they departed, without any promise of aid from Mr. Norris. The next morning, however, Mr. Norris said to Dr. Spring: "My wife tells me that this plan for a theological school and the missionary enterprise are the same thing. We must raise up the ministers if we would have the men go as missionaries." With this idea he promised to give $10,000 to found Andover Seminary. He went to the bank, drew out the whole amount in silver, carried it to his chamber, and with prayer dedicated it to the cause he loved. He explained his gift in silver by saying that "he had never heard that *paper* money was given to build the Temple." Who shall estimate the influence of those silver dollars? They have helped to educate three thousand ministers. They have helped to educate hundreds of missionaries, who have preached and taught, lived and died, for the heathen. They have gleaned in a path reaching from

Andover hill round the globe to Andover hill, — like the path of the just, which shineth more and more unto the perfect day.

But money may also be the most *lasting* power for good. Not only through all the world, but even through all time its influence may abide. For hundreds of years Oxford and Cambridge Universities have existed. For their endowment kings and queens were glad to contribute. Henry IV., Edward VI., Mary, Elizabeth, and Charles I. gave of their rich bounty. The august rulers of England, whose dust has mingled with native dust, still rule in the kingdom of scholarship. Here on these shores John Harvard and John Winthrop and Saltonstall and Yale endowed colleges. Funds are still held in trust by Harvard University which have for two hundred and fifty years made an education possible to youths whose brains were as large as their purses were small. From generation to generation, as men have come and men have gone, these benefactions have remained, and have dropped their showers of honorable aid.

In benevolence much money is so used as to be more useless than spilled water. It is the nurse of indolence and of crime. The Middle Ages were distinguished for their benevolence. The begging friars overran Europe; but they came as the locusts upon Egypt, to devour and to flee. But few results equal to the amount expended appeared. The relief was temporary. Money is not to be spent in loaves of bread to toss to a man in a bog; it is to be spent in a plank to get him out of the mire, that he may himself earn bread. Money, to be the means of the greatest good, must be so placed as to make its benefits *lasting;* and money may be so placed that its benefits shall last as long as eternity. The individual dies. His money may never die; it may last as long as there are woes to relieve, needs to supply, hearts to regenerate, souls to save. His money may be as an enduring character to remain on the earth to continue the work which he himself began.

Wealth represents the highest values.

What are they? They are intelligence, virtue, honor, truth, duty, character. Wealth is to be used in the fostering of these elements and ideals. The men and the society that are blessed with riches should be more intelligent, more honorable, more loyal to truth and to duty, and more just in the regard paid to human character than those not thus blessed. To the creation of these highest values wealth should be devoted.

This nation is rich. It is the wealthiest nation on the face of the globe. It has a future of material grandeur which exceeds the brightest pictures of fancy. Wealth nearly doubles every decade. In 1850 the real and personal property of the United States was seven billions; in 1860 it had increased to sixteen billions; in 1870 it had become twenty-four billions; in 1880 it was forty-three billions. It increases six millions every twenty-four hours. With this vast increase of vast wealth, the question becomes of mighty importance : Are these billions to be devoted to the service of God or to the service of Satan? In San Francisco are forty millionnaires, and only one is said to be a member of an evangelical church. Shall the wealth of this country be in the hands of godly or of ungodly men?

The old motto was, *Noblesse oblige*, — Nobility of blood binds one to noble service. The new motto is, *Richesse oblige*, — Riches bind one to noble service.

CHAPTER XII.

THE REWARDS OF CHRISTIAN WORK.

TO the members of every working church, as to every pastor, in the midst of wearying toil, frequently recurs the question: "What is the reward, what is the compensation?" The answer should always be free from utilitarian considerations. Every Christian laborer needs to inspire himself with the thought that the noblest rewards are his.

To the Christian one such compensation lies in the assurance that he is co-operating with the best forces of mankind, — he is putting himself in the line of the operation of the highest and most lasting powers of humanity. He is a part of that which makes for righteousness. He is one in that body of noble laborers which creates the best history.

He is one in that line of true men who receive the ball of progress and hand it on to those who come after. It is only the Christian whose life and work are thus embodied in the noblest forces of the race. I acknowledge the cultured learning, the high wisdom, and the literary genius of a Goethe; but I cannot forget that the pathway of Goethe was like the pathway of the lightning, brilliant and destructive. I acknowledge the pure aims, the unstinted generosity, the calm judgment of Harriet Martineau; but I cannot forget that her last years were devoted to a so-called science which, without lifting mortals to the skies, does not succeed in drawing angels down, — the science of Spiritualism. I acknowledge, and acknowledge with pleasure, the active philanthropies and the healthful reforms which are born and nurtured beyond the pale of the Church. Those who thus labor have their reward: it is the reward of putting their lives and operations in the line of those forces which work for righteousness. But in a degree higher, in a meaning nobler, does a Christian put his life into the work which elevates mankind. It is only the Christian aim which provides an ideal high enough for man. It is only the Christian motives which furnish strength sufficient for permanent activity. It is only the Star of Bethlehem which guides men to the shrine of purest worship. In the crypt of the old cathedral at Glasgow, facing toward the statue of John Knox, is a window with a picture of the Good Samaritan, and above it these words, in broad Scotch: " Let the deed shaw." So the Christian can say that his life, his work, are to *shaw*. In his life, in his work in relieving the evils of the race, in giving light for darkness, joy for sorrow, he has his compensation.

One may say that his life is a small life, that his work is a slight work. Say it if one will; but I also say that great results may flow from a life apparently small, from a work apparently slight. At one time the history of Europe depended upon the question whether the look-out man upon Nelson's

vessel would or would not descry a ship of
Napoleon's expedition to Egypt which was
passing not far off. "What shall we have?"
An aching head, a heavy heart, a weary
back; "many a sorrow, many a labor, many
a tear." "What shall we have?" If we
have wound-prints in our hands and feet, if
we have a crown of thorns, they are only
what He had. "What shall we have?"
We shall also have what He had, — the consciousness that our arm is striking strongest
blows against evil, that our hands are lifting
high the standard of the right. "Would you
see his monument, look about you!" are
words written concerning Sir Christopher
Wren on the walls of St. Paul's in London.
Is there any compensation of Christian service more sweet or more precious than the
assurance that we are working with the best
forces in the world for the improvement of
the race?

No petition is more frequent in the heart
of the faithful pastor than this prayer that
he may make his character of the greatest

worth. He would sell his life as dearly as possible; he would spill his blood, drop by drop; he would use heart and brain to the utmost. But he asks for himself no higher compensation than the consciousness that his prayer is answered, and that he is spilling his blood, drop by drop, in the fight for the faith.

A further compensation of Christian service, belonging both to the church, the pastor, and the individual, is the assurance that one is working with God. A faithful pastor can bear the loss of popularity, can endure the loss of the personal love of the church, can see pews emptied and income decrease; but he can see all this with a braver heart than he can see that his church is failing in its personal consecration, thus failing to give itself to the work of God for the world.

At Williamstown a single granite monument marks the spot where fourscore years ago stood a haystack, kneeling in whose shelter five college boys consecrated themselves to foreign missions. It is the birthplace of the foreign missionary work of the American Church. I follow those boys and other missionaries of our great century. The Asiatic cholera smote Gordon Hall and Samuel Newell, and their dust lies mingled with the coral sands of India. Adoniram Judson was buried at sea. Samuel J. Mills found an ocean grave on the coast of Africa.

Say, if one will, if one is so narrow and hard-hearted, that their lives knew no peace and satisfaction ; but one cannot long reflect on their work without knowing the deep compensations of their lives. They had builded their lives, they had builded their bodies, into the temple of God on earth, — a temple within whose walls the nations are to be gathered. They had laid down their lives as stepping-stones in the brook of time, that on them the Son of Man might walk in His triumphant progress round the world. Thus to build and thus to be were compensation sufficient.

We ask, Was Christ's life happy or unhappy, joyous or sad? It seems to me that it must have been a life in which both joy and sadness were more complete than in that of any other man. No one of Christ's insight into human nature, of Christ's tender heart, could live thirty-three years without seeing the sufferings of our poor, fallen, suffering humanity. Do you not think that He who saw and felt all the anguish and woe and sorrow of human hearts must have been sad and sorrowful? We never read of His smiling; we do read of His weeping. I think He must also have wept many silent tears. But do you not think that compensations of infinite worth were also His? What if one could go down to the pestilential parts of the great towns and say to the hungry, suffering, maimed, perishing bodies and souls, " Come to me ; I will give you what you most need," would not his heart be full of the deepest and richest and completest joy? This was Christ's power. This power must have been the source of joy. He could give, He wanted to give, He did give to all just so far as they were willing to receive what each most needed. His work was simply the work of man and of God, — the work of the God-man for the redemption of the world. His life must have been a life of the supremest joy and satisfaction.

In the feudal period of the Middle Ages, when a young man was to be made a knight, the attendants clothed him in a white tunic, a symbol of purity ; in a red robe, a symbol of the blood which he was bound to shed in the service of the faith ; in a toga, — a close black coat, — a symbol of the death which awaited him as well as all men. They put on his coat of mail, bound on his spurs, and girded on his sword. With his helmet on his brow, brandishing his lance, he went forth to war in the contest of chivalry. Imprisonment, suffering, death, might await him ; honor and fame and station might be his reward : but if he were a true chevalier, his deepest compensation would be the assurance that he was fighting for the faith with all his might, and that a hundred deaths were a bauble compared to his loyalty to his Divine Master and Lord. We recognize the compensations of the passive Christian virtues. We remember the eighth chapter of Romans. We know that like the anchor to the ship is this assurance that all things work together for good to the believer. We know that confidence which is founded upon the truth that "every man's life is a plan of God." We know the blessedness of seeing the love of God as revealed in the cross of Christ. They are all rich blessings and heavenly rewards of Christian service. But we would first give to men a richer compensation, the compensation of the service itself. "Behold, we have left all and followed thee." The following is the reward. Every faithful Christian can well say: "My Lord, in His work among men for God, suffered. If in my work He calls me to suffer, in that suffering may I find compensation. My Lord knew His Gethsemane. If I also have a Gethsemane, there, in the night and the cold and the loneliness, too, may I find my compensation. My Lord was crucified. If I am also nailed to some cross, in the very agony of death may I find compensation : all, all in the assurance that the suffering, the dark Gethsemane, and the cross are the ways in which I work with God in His labors for the redemption of the world."

CHAPTER XIII.

IN THE COUNTRY TOWN.

WE know that the population of the city increases faster than the population of the country. One-fourth of the people of the United States now live in cities. The proportional increase of the urban over the rural population has given the impression that the population of the city may be absolutely larger than the population of the country. Yet it is the truth that three-fourths of all the people of the United States live in the country. Important as is Christian work in the city, it is, therefore, more important in the country.

Advantages and difficulties, diverse and many, as to Christian work in the country are evident.

Among the elements favorable to Christian work in the country is the fact that the people in the country have homes; the people in the city are in boarding-houses. The institution of the family is favorable to the institution of the church. The relations of parenthood and childhood conduce to the formation of the best elements of character. These relations promote honesty, purity, self-sacrifice and love, elements which are at once the causes and the results of the work of the church. The boarding-house tends to the disintegration of the domestic relations, a disintegration unfavorable to the growth of the church and to permanent activity in Christian service.

With the more domestic life of the country is linked also a freedom from social engagements which is favorable to Christian work. Parties, amusements, are more common in the city. They use up time and strength, physical and intellectual. Those Christian people who indulge much in them find that so much of their power is subtracted from their power for engaging in Christian work.

The country, moreover, offers more leisure for thinking and reading than the diverse life of the city. The country reads proportionately more books and fewer papers; the city reads proportionately more papers and fewer books. The country proportionately thinks more and talks less; the city proportionately thinks less and talks more. This leisure and better cultivation furnish at once the ground for the doing of Christian work, and the agency in its doing.

It is evident that Sunday is better observed in the country than in the town. The fact needs only statement. The meaning of the fact, however, is significant. For Sunday is not simply a day of rest and worship, it is also a day best fitted for the doing of Christian work. Men are free from their ordinary toil. The time which they thus recognize as holy is conducive to Christian thinking and Christian activity. It is well to fill the hours of Sunday with Christian service.

An advantage which the country church

possesses over the urban relates to the greater homogeneousness of its membership and of its community. Of the three classes of persons who make up the community—those engaged in producing goods, those engaged in the distribution of goods, and those engaged in personal service—the producers are by far the larger part, and are found in the country. The population of the country is thus more homogeneous. In the whole nation, moreover, one person in every five is a member of an evangelical church; in the city, only one in thirteen. In the city of Chicago only one in nineteen is a member of an evangelical church. In Cincinnati the proportion is only one in twenty-three. It is not unusual in many metropolitan churches not to find a single workingman. But in the country workingmen compose the membership. Workingmen are at once the best material for the church to work on, and also the best agency for the church to work with. They are representative. The nation is composed on

the whole of workingmen, and not of lawyers or bankers. They are, moreover, by
intellectual nature clear-sighted, by moral
nature earnest, in method direct and persistent. The pastor may, as a rule, find his
best helpers among workingmen.

Allied to this homogeneousness of membership in church and community is the
fact that in the country no antagonism
against the church prevails. Such antagonism is found in the city. The Anarchist
and the Socialist are opposed to the church.
Some workingmen of the city are often
violent in antagonism to the church. The
church, they feel, represents wealth and
capital. But the country church, being
composed of workingmen, is, of course, free
from this antagonism.

A further element, constituting an advantage for Christian work in the country,
lies in the fact that the country church
occupies a larger place in the thought of its
members than the city church in the
thought of its members. This is not a

universal rule, for it is probable that the efficient church in the city, composed of the less well-to-do classes, does more for its members, and possibly more through its members, than any church of any other sort or constitution.

Moreover, to the church in the country most of its members turn not only for religious instruction and inspiration, but also for social and literary enjoyment and profit. As religion seems to occupy a larger place in the thought and life of country people than in the thought and life of the urban population, so also the church of the country which represents religion occupies a larger place.

All these elements, so diverse, I suggest as advantages which the country church has as a working church over its sister church in the metropolis.

But if the country church has these advantages it also suffers by reason of certain difficulties. The country church is usually not so well supplied with trained workers

as the city church. The training-schools
for Christian service are found in the
metropolis. The Young Men's Christian
Associations, with their classes for instruction, do not usually exist in country villages.
The churches are more and more inclined
to use workers who have that skill which
is not simply the result of Christian birth,
but of vigorous, intellectual and spiritual
training.

Such trained workers are frequently young
men and young women. Young men and
women are inclined to desert their country
homes and establish themselves in the city.
The church in the country thus suffers not
only from lack of material to work on, but
also from a lack of agency.

The urban population is more compact;
the country scattered. Solidarity of the
people tends to give effectiveness to Christian work as to work of every kind. The
same amount of work of the same quality
becomes more efficient in the city than in
the country. With this compactness of

population is to be joined, as an advantage possessed by the city, the element of enthusiasm. Enthusiasm for Christian service is important. Enthusiasm is aroused more easily among a thousand than among a hundred, among a hundred than among ten, persons.

The churches of the city, moreover, have more money to put into Christian work than the churches of the country. Money, while never to be sought for or used as an end, is ever to be sought for and used as a means, and the money which the Christian church possesses may prove a most effective means in accomplishing Christian aims. And yet it should be said, that if the city church has more money, the money in the country church is probably more evenly distributed, and such equality of distribution is an advantage for the steadiness and permanence of Christian service.

It is also to be added that in the city the spirit of denominationalism is probably less strong than in the country. The spirit of denominationalism may tend, and frequently does contribute, to the upbuilding of the churches of some one denomination. But the spirit of denominationalism does not tend, much less contribute, to the upbuilding of all churches or to the accomplishment of Christian aims. For the spirit of denominationalism is marked by apparently Jesuitical methods, and is usually characterized by a pettiness approaching meanness and by a selfishness nothing less than sinful. The city church in the struggle for existence, or for vigorous progress, is prone to embody too strongly the spirit of denominationalism; but the rural church meets the temptation usually in a yet stronger form.

Such are some of the advantages and disadvantages possessed by the working church of the country.

The methods which the church in the country should adopt are not far to seek. They lie along the line of public services, such as preaching, Sunday-schools, prayer-meetings, and visiting from house to house. But there is one method which the country church should adopt, exceedingly important in itself and not difficult of employment. For the sake of clearness in statement let me combine my principle and my illustration.

The town of F. contains three thousand people, one thousand in the village at the center, and two thousand lying outside, mainly farmers. Not one-tenth of those living outside of the village come to the churches in the village; and there are no churches outside the village. Four churches are in the village, doing the ordinary work for their constituency. The problem is: What can these churches do for those living outside the village bounds? The best method, it seems to me, is for the four pastors of these four churches to confer and decide that they will serve as pastors for the whole town. Let them, if they wish, divide the town, by geographical lines, into four districts, and each make himself the pastor of one district. Let each visit from house to house in his section. Let each organize Sunday-schools in the school-houses of each part. Let each establish a mid-week service in the school-houses. Let each, so far as possible, make himself the best pastor to his rural constituency. Such a method would insure the evangelization of the whole township.

But it may be objected, and the objection has more ground than it ought to have, that four pastors either could not, or would not, join in such united and devoted work. In such an instance I should suggest that one pastor consider himself the pastor of the whole town. Let him regard his parish in the light of the old parish system, making his church territory coterminous with the town territory. Let him, through his church, organize Sunday-schools in each school district. Let him, either in person or through members of the church, visit from house to house. Let him, through every possible means and method, bear the gospel of Christ to those that are without. Such a method is simple in conception, simple in execution, and, applied with ordinary wisdom and enthusiasm, would result in bearing the gospel to every soul.

INDEX.

———◆———